The Extensive Hip Hop Rhyming
Dictionary

Love,

mom
& Dad
xxo
Dec. 2016.

THE
EXTENSIVE
HIP HOP RHYMING DICTIONARY

By Gio Williams
Bull City Publishing, LLC
www.Bullcitypublishing.com

Hip Hop (hĭp′hŏp′) *n.* The popular culture of big-city and esp. inner-city youth, characterized by graffiti art, break dancing, and rap music[1].

Homonym (hŏm′ə-nĭm′) *n.* One of two or more words that have the same sound and often the same spelling but differ in meaning[2].

Rap (răp′) *n.* A form of popular music characterized by spoken or chanted rhyming lyrics with a syncopated, repetitive rhythmic accompaniment. **rapped, rapper, rap-ping, raps**[3].

Rhyme (rīm) *n.* **1.** A Correspondence of terminal sounds of words or of lines of verse. **2.** A word that corresponds with another in terminal sound. **rhymed, rhym-ing, rhymes**[4].

Table of Contents

Introduction

Welcome to the first Extensive Hip Hop Rhyming Dictionary. In this volume, we will provide you with a very brief introduction to the history of Rap and Hip Hop. This dictionary will provide the reader with the knowledge of different types of rhymes and illustrate the practice of these rhymes with examples from a variety of different artists. In the final chapters of this book, a multitude of common phrases will provide the reader with rhymes that go far beyond the basic *end rhyme*.

The objective of this dictionary is to provide writers with a perspective different from most rhyming dictionaries. Too often rhyming dictionaries provide very simple, monosyllabic rhymes that neglect to expand the mind and leave many works at the beginner-stage. Furthermore, an additional dictionary offers Homonym rhymes, which will be explained later in this book. Continue reading and take yourself to the next level.

A Brief History of Rap and Hip Hop

Before there was Rap or Hip Hop, there were the griots. Griots are West African poets and singers who traveled in groups, centuries before the 1700s. The music that was sung and developed by the griots is very similar and evocative of Hip Hop. Naturally, in that case, Hip Hop has its roots in African-American and West African music.

As the griots were a poetic folk, Rap developed into and combination of speech, poetry and song. It has been said that Rap is simply poetry with a beat. Although it is a word in itself, it could appear as an acronym. Common acronymic associations include "**R**hythm **a**nd **p**oetry," "**R**apping **a**bout **p**oetry," "**R**hythmic **A**frican **p**oetry," or "**R**hythmically **a**ssociated **p**oetry."

Notwithstanding, these groups of traveling musicians had a great impact on modern-day Rap; it took New York by storm. By the 1960s and 1970s Hip Hop rose and spread like wildfire through the cities of New York, particularly the Bronx. By the late 70s, the genre was spitting out DJs, MCs, break-dance, graffiti-art, and the manipulation of sounds and records through the use of turntables. Nevertheless, it continued developing and contemporary artists began adding their own styles and trademarks to distinguish themselves from others, but also to keep the culture alive and moving forward.

By the 1980s, the Hip Hop culture became a worldwide influence, which took it further in the 1990s and made it a mainstream form of music. Today Rap and Hip Hop are arguably the most listened to forms of music, taking their inception from West Africa and to the rest of the world as the most popular musical genre.

Different Types of Rhymes

Rhymes come in many forms and can be used through a variety of techniques. In this chapter, we will explain the different types of rhymes that can be used interchangeably, and with incredible effect.

END RHYME

Also known as a TERMINAL RHYME. This is the most common rhyme pattern. End rhymes rhyme the end words of a line. Additionally, end rhymes can be found in two consecutive lines, alternate lines, or even in more distant lines.

> *We don't get down like **that**/*
> *Lay my game down quite **flat**[5]/*
>
> - *Notorious B.I.G. (I Got a Story to Tell)*

INTERNAL RHYME

Also known as a MIDDLE RHYME. Internal rhymes are also used frequently and occur when a rhyme exists within a single line. Internal rhymes are very effective in adding emphasis and speeding up the pace of the rhythm.

> *I see no **changes** all I see is **racist faces**/*
> *Mis**placed** **hate** **makes** dis**grace** to **races**[6]/*
>
> - *Tupac (Changes)*

FULL RHYME

Also known as an ORDINARY RHYME. A full rhyme constitutes two words that sound exactly the same, except for the primary consonant sound.

> *Though I can't let you **know** it/*
> *pride won't let me **show** it[7]/*
>
> *— Jay Z (Song Cry)*

IMPERFECT RHYME

Also known as a HALF RHYME, NEAR RHYME, SLANT RHYME, OFF RHYME, PARTIAL RHYME, CONSONANTAL RHYME or PARARHYME. Imperfect rhymes are suggestive of rhyme; however fail to meet the criterion that constitutes a rhyme. In these rhymes, consonants may sound similar and very commonly the final consonant is identical. However, vowels do not and thus the effects of the imperfect rhyme provide a slightly dissonant result.

> *Words were weapons against **their hate**/*
> *Shepherds search for stars in **her hair**[8]/*
>
> *— Nas (The Outcome)*

VISUAL RHYME

Also known as a SIGHT RHYME, EYE RHYME or COURTESY RHYME. Visual rhymes look alike and would appear to rhyme, but do not.

> ***One**/ **Bone**/*
> ***Love**/ **Move**/ **Drove**/*
>
> *— n. author*

MASCULINE RHYME

Also known as a STRONG RHYME. All monosyllabic rhymes are in theory masculine rhymes. By definition, a masculine rhyme occurs on emphasized syllables. When rhyming two or more syllables, the rhyme is masculine if the final syllable is stressed.

> *For the case to race with a chance*
> *to face the **judge**/*
> *And I'm guessing my soul won't*
> ***budge**[9]/*

> *- Bone Thugs-N-Harmony (Crossroads)*

FEMININE RHYME

Also known as a WEAK RHYME or DOUBLE RHYME. Feminine rhymes relate to rhymes where the final syllable is not emphasized.

> *And it's absurd, how people hang on*
> *every word/*
> *I'll probably never get the props I*
> *feel I ever **des**erve/*
> *But I'll never be served, my spot is*
> *forever **res**erved/*
> *If I ever leave earth, that would be*
> *the death of me first[10]/*

> *- Eminem (Till I Collapse)*

POLYSYLLABIC RHYME

Polysyllabic rhymes correspond only in the final syllable or syllables. This form of rhyming will call attention to it and is heavily emphasized.

> Never thinking 'bout the
> consequences of her **actions**/
> Living for today and not tomorrow's
> satis**faction**[11]/

> - Ludacris (Runaway Love)

TRIPLE RHYME

In triple rhyme, the rhyme places emphasis on one syllable, followed by a lack of emphasis on the two following syllables[12].

> We sell, **crack** to our own out the
> **back** of our homes[13]/

> - Talib Kweli (Get By)

ALLITERATIVE RHYME

Alliteration is a very powerful technique used often in rhyme that should not go unused and will not go unnoticed. By using the same consonant or vowel repeatedly, a strong effect can be created, heightening the power of the particular line and speeding up the pace of the rhyme.

> Might bite the mic while I try to write
> tighter/

> - n. author

The Homonym Dictionary

Homonyms are often overlooked given the similar spelling and pronunciation deters writers from using them. It is possible that homonymic rhymes are further overlooked because writers do not think to use them. In either case, it is recommended to stay away from this paradigm because homonyms can be used with great power and effect as well when delivered correctly.

A

Ad – Add
Ail – Ale
Air – Heir
Are - R
Ate - Eight
Aye - Eye - I

B

B – Be - Bee
Base - Bass
Bi – Buy - By – Bye
Bite - Byte
Boar - Bore
Board - Bored

C

C – Sea - See
Capital – Capitol
Chord - Cord
Coarse – Course
Core - Corps
Creak – Creek
Cue – Q - Queue

D

Dam - Damn
Dawg - Dog
Days - Daze
Dew - Do - Due
Die - Dye
Dual - Duel

E

Earn - Urn
Elicit - Illicit
Elude - Illude
Ex - X

F

Fat - Phat
Faze - Phase
Feat - Feet
Find - Fined
Flea - Flee
Forth - Fourth

G

Gait - Gate
Genes - Jeans
Gnawed - Nod
Grate - Great

H

Hair - Hare
Heal - Heel
Hear - Here
Heard - Herd
Hi - High
Higher - Hire
Hoarse - Horse
Hour - Our

I

Idle - Idol
Ill - Ill
In - Inn
Inc - Ink
IV - Ivy

J

Juggler - Jugular

K

Knead - Need
Knew - New
Knight - Night
Knot - Naught - Not
Know - No
Knows - Nose

L

Lead - Led
Lie - Lie
Light - Lite
Loan - Lone

M

Mach - Mock
Made - Maid
Mane - Main
Meat - Meet
Might - Mite
Mouse - Mouth

N

Naval - Navel
None - Nun

O

Oar - Or - Ore
One - Won

P

Paced - Paste
Pail - Pale
Pair - Pear
Peace - Piece
Peak - Peek
Peer - Pier
Pray - Prey

Q

Quarts - Quartz

R

Rain - Reign
Rap - Wrap
Read - Red
Real - Reel
Right - Write
Ring - Wring

S

Scene - Seen
Seas - Sees - Seize
Sole - Soul
Some - Sum
Son - Sun
Steal - Steel
Suite - Sweet

T

T - Tee
Tail - Tale
Team - Teem
Their - There - They're
Thyme - Time
To - Too - Two

U

U - You

V

Vale - Veil
Vain - Vane - Vein
Vary - Very
Verses - Versus

W

Waive - Wave
Ware - Wear - Where
Wait - Weight
Waist - Waste
Which - Witch
Why - Y
Wood - Would

X

Y

Yoke - Yolk
Yore - Your - You're

Z

The Extensive Hip Hop Rhyming Dictionary

The remainder of this book is devoted purely to the Rhyming Dictionary. First, explanations will be offered with respect to the dictionary, as well as suggestions to the use of the common phrases and the dictionary. Common phrases are provided under their respective alphabetical letters, starting with numerical associations.

N.B.1
Each rhyme matches the number of syllables following the common phrase. However, there are cases where the syllable count does not match. In these instances, the syllables that are outside of the common phrase count are underlined. For example, see an excerpt below.

Must be right <u>Ad</u>just the light

In this model, the "<u>Ad</u>" is underlined while the "just the <u>light</u>" remains within the syllable count of the common phrase.

N.B.2
In some instances, the rhymes end with words that may not properly complete a sentence, punch line, line, etc. In these instances, the flow and/or delivery can always be switched up and carried over to the next line. For example, see an excerpt below, including a sample.

Feel regret People get

In this example, *People get* can be a full-stop, or can be continued to the next line.

  I'll deliver my rhymes and never *feel regret/*
  And I'm not one to lie, but that's how *people get/*

  -

  I'll deliver my rhymes and never *feel regret/*
  And I'm not one to lie, but that's how *people get/*
  sometimes...

In these samples, it is possible to see how the common phrase and the rhyme can be used in two different ways. As a writer, it is essential to think outside of the box as there will always be more than one way to deliver a line.

N.B.3

Lines in music are generally delivered colloquially. This implies that the speech-delivery is different from the text. For example, as opposed to reciting *Living it up*, many writers will deliver it as *Livin' it up*. With that in mind, this dictionary provides the formally written text, and leaves it up to the reader to deliver it as he/she deems appropriate.

Additionally, conjunctions have been created that do not exist in the English language to express spoken prose. For example, see below.

So is has been combined to create *So's*

Rhyme will has been combined to create *Rhyme'll*

Is not has been combined to create *Ain't*

N.B.4

The majority of rhymes in this dictionary focus on syllable assonance. The rhymes provided below may require different syllable emphasis or different flow delivery. Readers are reminded that as writers and artists, you have a poetic license allowing you to be distinct, distinguishable and make the writing work for itself, even if it means pulling words out of thin-air. If everything sounded the same, there would be no variety, no exclusivity and all forms of music, rhyme and delivery would be imitable. Readers should avoid the fear to be different.

N.B.5

Rhymes provided are left to interpretation. Originally, rhymes standing alone may not be clear. However, when added at the end of a sentence these rhymes can be used powerfully and will cease to be obscure. For example, please see below concerning the respective common phrase.

Power play Crown away

Originally, *crown away* on its own does not appear to have any meaning. However, when used in the following context, *power play* and *crown away* create a meaningful rhyme.

A team on my own, deliver like a *power play/*

Call the king of rap, you can't take the *crown away/*

N.B.6

By no means is this rhyming dictionary exhaustive. Readers are encouraged to add rhymes to the common phrases, or if necessary, replace certain words with others! For example, *Run and hide* can be changed to *Run or hide.*

Additionally, a variety of word endings can be substituted in the rhymes provided in the dictionary. It is important to stress the fact that what is offered as rhyme alternatives, is not set in stone.

> Word endings that can be lengthened and maintain one syllable count include:
> *-s,* **-ed**

> Word endings that can be lengthened, but will increase the rhyme by an additional syllable count include:
> *-ies, -ing,* **-ed***, -er, -es, -ment, -ive, -ion, -al*

* Please note that certain endings can be exchanged with others, therefore not increasing the syllable count. The word ending "-ed" has been highlighted in bold as it may increase or maintain the same syllable count depending on the context, and word(s) used.

123

123

Come through me, Come to be, Come to me, Done with me, Dumb to see, Hum with me, Lunch for free, Monkey tree, Run quick see, Run to me, Run with me, Some do see, Undo me, Unto thee

411

For someone, Fortune's come, Fortune's dumb, Scorching sun, Sore tongue's dumb, Sort of dumb

24/7

Any more heavens, Many more devils

911

Bite some gum, Blind and dumb, Find someone, Lines are done, Nine to one, Signed and done, Time has come, Time to run

50-50

Hit the city, In a jiffy, It's a mystery, It's at fifth street, Missed me-Missed me, Pretty nifty, This is history, This is nifty, This is shifty

0 percent

Below the fence, Be so against, Feel no regret, Feel so depressed, Free to defend, Leave through the vent, Need no amends, We close the end, We know the rest

1 percent

Come or went, Must amend, Must avenge, Must defend, Rush the end, Summer went, Up the bend, Underwent

2 percent
Came through and went, Due for rent, Lose a cent, Lose the scent, New defense, Through the fence, To lament, Who's against

10 percent
Best defense, Decadent, Detriment, Elegant, Element, Evident, Left a dent, Left and went, Left a scent, Meant the end, Testament

30 percent
Earning a cent, Hurting again, Learning to vent, Were different, Word isn't meant

50 percent
60 percent, Is different, Is imminent, It will depend, Within the pen

80 percent
Came in and went, Facing the lens, Making amends, Making the rent, Playing against, Race in the Benz, Retaliate and avenge,

90 percent
Might be against, Time came and went, Time isn't spent, Tiny and dense, Try to amend, Write with the pen,

100 percent
Come to an end, Hunger's intense, It's under torrent, Mustn't pretend, The thunder relents, Under the fence

1 time
Fun rhyme, Lunch line, Punch line, Run mine, Sometime, Sunshine, Unwind, Won mine,

2 times
Loose lines, Lose mine, New rhymes, Shoe shine, Too fine, Too kind, Too tight, True mind

3 times

Be fined, Rewind, Resign, Benign, Be mine, Knee high, Feline, Seize time, Least time, Breeze by, Free lines, Keep rhyming

4 times

More crime, More rhymes, Old times, Report signed, Shoreline, Short lines, Short mind, Soar high, Storm rise

5 times

Buy time, Fly by, Guidelines, Hide mine, High five, High tide, I shine, Light shines, Limelight, Line rhymes, Might shine, My lines, Nine lives, Sidelines, White lies

6 times

Fistfight, Fix mine, It's fine, Pick mine, Sick rhymes, Skintight, Spit shine, Slick rhyme, This high, This time, Which line, With rhymes

7 times

Better eyes, Better lives, Ever try, Every line, Get behind, Heaven lies, Set the style, Well and fine, Wet and dry

8 times

Bass line, Great rhyme, Hate crimes, Lakeside, Make signs, Race line, State line, Statewide, Take mine, Taste fine

9 times

Buy time, Fly by, Guidelines, Hide mine, High five, High tide, I shine, Light shines, Limelight, Line rhymes, Sidelines, Might shine, My lines, Nine lives, White lies

10 times

Can rhyme, Can find, Hence why, Left signs, Pen writes, Then try, When's fine

20 times

Gemini, Get behind, Get in line, Let me try, Many lines, Plenty rhymes, When it's mine, When it's time, Very fine

50 times

Busy night, Busy times, Give me mine, Hit rewind, Shifty crime, Sicker rhymes, Silly lines, Spit and shine, Still in mind

100 times

Come and find, Cuddle time, Subtle lines, Summer time, Underlined, Wasn't mine, What a rhyme, What's the crime

First

Birth, Curse, Earth, Hurts, Lurch, Mirth, Perch, Search, Surf, Third, Turf, Words, Worse, Worth, Verse

Second

Beckoned, Bet in, Betting, Dead end, Deadened, Depend, Descend, Get in, Getting, Reckoned, Set in, Setting, Reddened

Third

Absurd, Bird, Birth, Curse, Earth, Hurts, Lurch, Mirth, Nerd, Occurred, Perch, Referred, Search, Surf, Third, Turf, Verse, Word, Worse, Worth

Fourth

Coarse, Course, Force, Forth, Hoarse, Horse, Pores, Source, Torch, Wars

Abide by
> A drive by, A dry eye, A fly guy, Denied by, I might try, So bye-bye, The tide's high

Above and beyond
> A drug to be on, Among other songs, Another eon, The blood is a bond, The struggle is long, To love and be gone

Absolute power
> Back in an hour, Back to you cowards, Rap it for hours, Shackle and cower, Stack like a tower, That is just sour

Absolute zero
> Attacking the hero, Blast at the ego, Rap is a credo, That's what you see though

Accept the fact
> Arrest the pack, A test to pass, Collect the cash, Dissect the track, Except for that, It set us back, The second act

Access denied
> Rap gets defied, The best is tried, That's left aside, That's testified

Ace is back
> Chase it fast, Face the bad, Lace the track, Mace attack, Make the cash, Place is at, State the fact, Stay with that, Take it back, Trace it back, Waste of that

Ace of bass

Ace of spades, Case to case, Face to face, Make them chase, Pace the race, Place to place, State to state, Take the case, Trace erased

Acid attack

Acting in tact, Ask for it back, Back in a flash, Back it to back, Gasping aghast, Half of a track, Last one to laugh, Master the track, Rap is intact

Act a fool

Acting cool, Acting cruel, Back to school, Plastic tool, That's a rule

A.D.D.

A.B.C., May be me, Maybe see, Pay to see, Play the beat, Rate is free, Say to me, Take a knee

Add that together

Pass past the weather, Rap's back forever, That's fact forever, That's plastic leather, That track is better

Adrenalin rush

A record to cut, A second to hush, Eleven's enough, I beckon the rush, I reckon enough, Seven and up, So settle the bunch, To meddle in stuff

Aftermath

Back to back, Blasting past, Cast a shadow, Faster cat, Grab the cash, Half of that, Last to laugh, Master rap, Master that, Past is passed, Scratch the rash, Stash the cash

Aftershock

Ask the cops, Astronaut, Back it tossed, Blasting off, Cast a rock, Crash a lot, Laughing stock, Pass the block, Rap is soft, That is hot, Trash is talk

Age of hip hop
Make a pit stop, Make a quick stop,
Make it criss cross, Make it tip top,
Making this stop, Take the lid off,
Play the big boss, Play the kick off

Age of rap
Crazy track, Face the fact, Make me
act, Play the track, Stay in back, Stay
intact, Take it back, Way in back

Ain't that right
Afraid of heights, Awake at night, Late
at night, Make that tight, Shade the
light, Trained to fight, Waive the
right

Ain't that the truth
Break back the tooth, Gave rap a boost,
Lame track produced Take back the
truce, Take rap to booths

All of the above
Call it summer love, Fall and get back
up, Halt the fallen blood, Salt is on
the slug

All or nothing
Call for something, Not disgusting,
Stop discussing, Wall is crushing

Alphabet
Ask to get, Back to debt, Cast a net,
Half the bet, Past the set

Ancient history
Make a mystery, Making history, Pain
and misery, Shame and infamy, Take it
with me

Answer this
Anarchist, Cancerous, Can dismiss,
Chance to miss, Chances with, Hand to
fist, Land of mist, Plan to miss,
Standing with

Any minute
    Can be in it, In a clinic, Let me
    finish, Let me spin it, Many mimic,
    Pennies in it
Any time, any place
    And in time will erase, Be surprised
    and amazed, Cannot find in the maze,
    Get in line in the race, Let me sign in
    the space, Many lines can erase,
    Redesigned and replaced
Apocalypse
    Approximate, Got some tricks, Got the
    fix, Not to quit, Stop and sit, Stop
    with it, Talking quick, The clock'll
    tick
Apocalyptic
    Amoxicillin, I'm optimistic, Stop to
    think if, The clock is ticking, The
    spots are filling, To stop assisting
Arm's length
    Ardent, Are dense, Are tense, Arson,
    Barbed fence, Car dent, Gardens,
    Hardens, Hard wrench, Heart's tense,
    Lost sense, Nonsense
Army of one
    Are we yet done, Barring someone,
    Calling it dumb, Far from the sun, Gnaw
    up the gum, Sorry it's done, Stars and
    the sun, Starting to hum
Around and around
    Bounce to the sound, Bound to the
    ground, Clowning around, Down to the
    ground, Found by the hounds, Hounding
    around, Round after round
Around the block
    Around the clock, Bound to drop, Down
    to rock, Found and lost, Found the
    lock, How to talk, How to walk, The
    ground is hot, The shouting stops

Art of rap
> Arson act, Barter that, Call a cab, Falling back, Far from that, Garter strap, Guard the back, Part of that, Starter cap, Start with that

Art of hip hop
> Charges get dropped, Part of it stops, Party did stop, Start to criss-cross, Start to get hot, Watch the pin drop

Art of rhyme
> All of mine, Call the time, Chart and climb, Got the sign, Hard to find, Solid line, Start the time

Ashamed to say
> Again today, A game to play, A later day, And sail away, A place to stay, Make the play, So say my name, Take away, The main array, To stay away

Ashes to ashes
> Back as elastic, Bad as a fascist, Bad at the practice, Bag it in plastic, Clasp and attach it, Clashing and crashing, Gather the masses, Passed and elapsed it, Rap isn't drastic, Thrash it and mash it, Wrap it in plastic

As of now
> Ask them how, Back it down, Back to town, Blast around, Blast the sound, Last to count, Mash the ground, Pass it out, Practice now

Asthma attack
> Ask for it back, Blast to the past, Drafted the fastest, Pass in the back, Platinum plaque, Tackle the track, That is a fact, That's in the bag

A to Z
> A to B, Major league, Maybe three, Pay to see, Play the beat, Say to me, Take a knee, Wait and see, Way to be

Automatic

All about it, Autocratic, Call an addict, Caught a bad hit, I'll look at it, Lots of static, Thought about it

Baby boy
> Made for joy, May annoy, May be coy, Play a ploy, Play with toys

Baby girl
> Made me whirl, Make it twirl, Make me hurl, Save the world, Take the world, Waves and curls

Back and forth
> Ask for more, Back on course, Crash with force, Half is more, Pass the torch, Track is coarse, Track the source, Track it north

Back door
> Adore, Ask for, Bad sore, Last for, Last four, Pastor, Last score, Rap for, Rap lord, Rap lore, Rap more, Trap door

Back it up
> Back with us, Laugh it up, Pack it up, Rack them up, Slash and cut, That's enough, That was luck

Back on track
> Ask to rap, Bad attack, Bad infraction, Cadillac, Crack the bat, Master rap, Rap attack, Stack the plaque, That was action, Track it back

Backstab
> Blast at, Fast track, Gasp at, Grasp that, Lack that, Last track, Nab that, Pass back, Passed that, That's rap, That's that

Back to back
Ask to rap, Crack the bat, Fast to act, Lack the knack, Master rap, Master that, Rap attack, Stack the plaques, That's an act, Track it back, Whack the bat

Back to fight
Ask to write, Bad tonight, Black and white, Blast the hype, Catch the light, Mastermind, Nasty sight, Pack it tight, That's a night, That was right

Back to the basics
Dabble and taste it, Last in the races, Laugh in the faces, Tackled and aced it, Tackle the cases, That isn't wasted, Track it and trace it

Back to work
After first, As of birth, Cash is first, Disaster lurks, Half the earth, Lack the thirst, That will hurt, That will work

Back track
Back pack, Bad act, Lack that, Rat pack, Sad fact, Sat back, That's that, That's whack

Back up
Bad cut, Bad luck, Bad stuff, Crack up, Rack up, Stack up, That's nuts, That's tough

Bad attitude
Backpacking through, Pack back into, That mad at you, That's acting rude, That's black and blue

Bad habit
Asthmatic, Back at it, Fast at it, Lash at it, Last at it, Rap addict, That's padded, That static

Balance of power

Back up and cower, Last for an hour, Patent what's ours, Practice for hours, Savage and sour, Talent is ours

Bandwagon

And action, Can happen, Can't happen, Fans laughing, Hands clapping, Pants sagging, Ran past them, Sand dragon, Stand back and

Bank on that

Abandon that, And the facts, Answer that, Banners flap, Banter back, Can't attack, Fans amass, Fans attack, Hands are back, Hands'll clap, Ran it back, Standing back

Barbed wire

Are admired, Bar fire, Call a liar, Car tire, Got fired, Got hired, Guards fired, Hot wire, Start a fire

Bare hands

Fair chance, Hair bands, Hair strands, Make plans, Square dance, Stare trance, Take stance, Their fans, Their plans

Bark back

Arch back, Art stack, Dart back, Far back, Hard rap, Part black, Sarcastic, Start clapping, Start that

Bark out loud

Called it out, Darken out, Hard to shout, Heart is proud, Sharper now, Smart and proud, Start to crowd, Start to route

Batter up

Add it up, Bad at luck, Bag it shut, Battle cut, Chat the smut, Mad and nuts, Saddle up

Battle of wits

Back at the tip, Haggle with it, Paralysis, Matter a bit, Rap is a cinch, Rattle a bit, Shackles are ripped, That is a trick

Bead of sweat

Beat the rest, Breathe and ex<u>hale</u>, Feel regret, Keep a set, Leave and let, Need to bet, Need to fret, People get, Seat is wet, Sweep the deck

Be a man

Decent hand, Even hands, Freeze the land, Keep a stance, Keep the fans, Lease a van, Piece of sand, We enhance

Beat the system

Cheap magician, Keep on wishing, People listen, People missing, See it glisten, See the vision, Speak of wisdom, Weak addition

Beg for mercy

Get the first thing, Getting dirty, Getting thirsty, Head for thirty, Lead dispersing, Let the girl be

Behind the scenes

Denied the dream, Dry and clean, Find a seat, In right between, In time will see, It's kind of mean, Remind the fiends, Rewind it please, The mind is keen, We like to dream, We might be seen

Believe this

A free wish, A peace wish, Decree this, Relieve with, So beat this, To feel bliss, To leave with

Below the belt

For show and tell, It's going well, So hope to sell, The flow is felt, Then go for help, Then go to hell, The slow are held, The soldier fell

Belt buckle
Befuddled, Felt fuddled, Felt trouble, Help struggle, Melt butter, Sell double, Then cuddle

Bend the rules
End the cruise, End the duels, Felt the blues, Get the clues, Get the jewels, Get the tools, Getting schooled, Lend the shoes, Tend to drool, Tend to lose

Best of the best
Fester the best, Get what is left, Just got arrested, Less than the rest, Mess with the rest, Set to the crest, Testing the tested

Better off
Bet is lost, Debt and losses, Get her off, Head is lost, Set it off, Settle costs, Settle lawsuits, Settle losses, Smell exhaust, Whether not

Big mouth
Dig out, Kick out, Miss out, Spit out, This house, This town, Without

Bird's eye
First try, Girl's cry, Heard why, Lurch by, Search high, Their size, Third try, Verse lies

Bite back
Buy that, Write raps, Type that, Tight track, Fight that, Like that, Nightcap, Ride that, Right track, Wide gap, Write that

Bite it off
Fight them off, Guide the block, High and posh, Higher cost, Kind of lost, Lighter knock, Like to rock, Pry the lock, Side and top, Time the clock, Try to rock, While it rots

Bit of this, bit of that
> If it hits hit it back, In the fist is the clap, In the mist is the fact, Kick it in Kick it back, Listen this isn't whack, Spit it quick in the rap

Bitter end
> Did again, In event, This offends, Until it mends, With a fence, With a friend, With a ten, With the pen, With the trend

Bittersweet
> In defeat, In the beat, In the street, Isn't neat, Mystery, Rip a sheet, Risen feat, Visit me, With a peep, With the key

Black and white
> Back tonight, That's alright, Pass the light, Rap delight, Half a mic, Crash the bike, Laugh and fight

Blank check
> Band set, Bank debt, Can't get, Grand theft, Handset, Tram wreck

Blindfolded
> I'll hold it, I sold it, I told it, Lights bolted, Mic told it, Time's stolen

Blink of an eye
> Lift it up high, Pink in the eye, Sink in the sky, Snivel and cry, Thinking to try, Think it'll fly, Think up a lie

Block buster
> Block hustle, Crop duster, Got flustered, Got hustled, Got tougher, Hot summer, Shots mustered

Block it out
> Lost without, Not without, Talk about, Talking loud, Talk or shout, Toss about, Walk it out, Walk around

Blood clot

Club spot, Love got, Mug shot, Thugs shot, Upshot

Blow to pieces

Flow the beat with, Go to be with, Hope to seize it, Know the reason, Know the thesis,

Borderline

Corner sign, For the rhyme, Lord of rhyme, More in time, Order nine, Overtime, Stormy time, Torture time,

Born winner

Bold sinner, Cold winter, For dinner

Boxing match

Got the fact, Hop in back, Lock and latch, Lost the match, Spot the facts, Shopping bag, Stop and catch, Stop the past, Talk and act

Brain freeze

Break dreams, Claim these, Lame tease, Main squeeze, Make cheese, Plain tee's, Say please, Spray grease, Take three

Brainwashed

Chains locked, Fame costs, Game's lost, Paint tossed, Same cost, Trains cross

Brake lights

Chain spikes, Daylight, Great sights, Hate fights, Late night, Make right, Pray tight, Stage fright, Tastes like

Breadwinner

Dead ringer, Dead winter, Get dinner, Get thinner, Head ringer, Lead filler

Break away

Chase and play, Chase away, Make a way, Make my day, O̲bey and stay, Play by play, Take a break, Take a day

Break even

Eight reasons, Late evening, Late season, Take freedom

Breathe in deep
Clean and neat, Feel it creep, Feel the beat, Feel the peace, Keep the seat, Leave the street, Reach the peak, Read between

Bridge together
Did it better, Did it clever, Is forever, Is it better, Isn't better, Lift the lever, Tickle feather

Bright light
Fight like, Fight night, Lime light, Mic writes, Might fight, Nightlight, Night sight, Sidelight, Write tight, Write trite

Bring it on
In a thong, In the dawn, Is it wrong, It is gone, Listen on, Sing along, With a song

Bring the noise
Drink the poi<u>son</u>, Lift and hoist, Listen boys, Singing voice, This annoys, This destroys, With the choice

Bring the heat
Cinch to speak, Fix the leak, Hindered speech, Hinges creak, In a week, In defeat, In the beat, In the street, Since a week, Sing the beat, Think to cheat

Bulletproof
Full of juice, Full of truth, Pull a spoof, Pull a tooth, Pulling loose, Pulling through, Pull it loose

Bumper to bumper
Hundreds of blunders, Hunted and hunter, Jump to another, Plunder for hunger, Pump up another, Run from the hunter, Summer to summer, Thunderous wonder, Under the jumper

Burning desire

Burning with fire, Burn with the fire, Learn to admire, Permit to fire, Searching to hire, Turning it higher, Turning the tire, Urn into fire

Burn the rubber

Discerning trouble, Earn another, Earning double, Her and others, Learn from others, Learn it brother, Turn to rubble, Turn to trouble

Bury the hatchet

Carry the basket, Get a bit drastic, Staring and gasping, Very elastic, Wear it and flash it

By any means

And he means, And it seems, I haven't seen, In any scene, My many dreams, With empty dreams, With plenty schemes

By the way

By today, Find a way, Lie away, Like to say, Pry away, Sigh and say, Sign the paper, Simon say, Try today, Try to play, Why today

Caged animal
>   Chain manacles, Made tangible, Razed mandibles, Stage manager, Takes stamina

Cage fighter
>   Hate spiders, Make cider, Make tighter, Page biter, Rage writer, Sage writer

Call for back-up
>   All the tracks cut, Call it bad luck, Fall get back up, Halls are backed up, Hard to catch up, Start to act up, Walls are stacked up, Wasn't that much

Call a bluff
>   All of us, All the luck, All the stuff, Brawn and rough, Fall and cut, Small and gruff, Tall and tough, Tall enough

Call the cops
>   All the stops, Call the shots, Fall a lot, Halt and stop, Halter top, On the spot, Parking lot, Pop the locks

Calm down
>   All round, Crawl round, Fall down, Stall down, Walls sound

Cancel out
>   And without, Answer now, Candles out, Dance about, Handle doubt, Stand to shout

Candle stick
>   And a bit, Cancel it, Dance a bit, Dance with it, Handle it, Handle this, Ran with it, Tangled with

Cannibalistic
>Chances to risk it, Hand in a biscuit, Land of the mystic, Man we ballistic, Planning to risk it, Slam it and whisk it

Cannon ball
>Animal, Ban it all, Land the call, Man the wall, Standing tall, Stand to fall

Can't believe it
>And receive it, Anti-thesis, Man just leave it, Plan to beat it, Plan to keep it

Can't stop
>And drop, And shot, Fans got, Hands caught, Hands drop, Sandlot, Stand top

Capital letters
>Faster than ever, Lasting forever, Master it better, Practice it better, Stack up the cheddar

Captivating
>Activating, Ashes fading, Back debating, Bad in ratings, Exasperating, Masquerading, Masticating, Rap is fading, Track and tracing

Cardboard box
>Bark or talk, Charcoal rocks, Hardcore block, Hardcore rock, Start to drop

Cardiac arrest
>Back to beat the rest, Back to be the best, Far from the best, Sorry that I left

Carnivore
>Charter for, Hard and sore, Harder core, Party more, Start to soar, Want it more

Carry the weight
>Bury the hate, Ferry will take, Hair in the face, Pair of an eight, Preparing

for fate, Stare in the face, Very innate, Very irate, Where is the bass

Carved in stone

All is known, All is shown, Call the phone, Darts are thrown, Far from home, Heart of stone, Start to drone, Starve alone

Case closed

Chase flows, Fake clones, Late shows, Make the most, Take both, Trace those, Waste those

Cash money

Bad tummy, Fast running, Raps runny, That dummy, That's funny

Catch my breath

Ask the rest, Blast the chest, Chapters left, Pass the test, Raps a mess, That's the best

Catch the beat

Blast the heat, Clash the street, Hat to feet, Mash your feet, Shackled feet, Stacks are neat, That's the street, Trash is cheap

Cause and effect

All that is left, Auction the rest, Boss of the rest, Hot off the press, Lost in the bet, Maul in the chest, Pause and eject, Rock it the best

Cause a riot

All deny it, Called a liar, Gnaw and bite it, Laws divide it, Pause rewind it, Stop to try it, Toss an eye in

Chain link

Game sinks, Fake ring, Main thing, Plaintiff, Skate rink, Stained ink, Tainted, Trained in, Wait think

Chain reaction

Blame the captain, Make it happen, Make it lasting, Pain is passing, Rain is passing, Take a fraction, Taking action

Chalk it out

Bark about, Blocking out, Darker out, Lock it out, Stalk around, Stalk the crowd, Start to shout, Talk about, Talk is loud

Change direction

Chair ejection, Late affection, Late detection, Pain infection, Range of section, Stage election, Take protection

Change of heart

Aced the art, Embrace the art, Make it start, Placed apart, Race the car, Take apart, Takes some smarts

Change the flow

Bass is low, Case is closed, Fake the O, Hate to go, Make it grow, Make it snow, Take it slow

Charged with

Barged in, Carpet, Car sick, Hard grip, Hard hit, Parked it, Tar pit

Checkmate

Chest plate, Deadweight, Headway, Help's late, Lead weight, Set ways, Test phase

Check it out

Chicken out, Deck it out, Get it out, Set the count

Childproof

Blind truth, Filed tooth, Fly through, Hide truth, Lied to, Rhyme spoof, Ride through, Style used, Tied noose, Tight noose

Child's play
>Guide way, I'll stay, Mile-away, Right way, Styles fade, Wild day

Choke hold
>Blow sold, Coke sold, Don't fold, Flow's cold, Flow's sold, Grow cold, Grow old, So cold

Chop it up
>Got it cut, Lock it up, Lost a buck, Lots of luck, Lots of smut, Pop a gut, Proper stuff

Chopped in half
>Bought the last, Got the cash, Got to laugh, Lost a half, Lost it fast, Rock it back, Stop and crash, Toss the trash

Chrome on the wheels
>Choked on the peel, Close on the deal, Close to the heel, Hope that it's real, Lonesome appeal, Most of us feel, Open to deal, Over the shield, Sober and real, Won't even steal

Class act
>Back pack, Bad act, Clap back, Fast track, Lack that, Rat pack, Sad fact, Sat back, That's that, That's whack

Classic rap
>Ask for that, Back to back, Drastic tact, Magic act, Master tactics, Master that, Pass it back

Clear the mind
>Beer or wine, Fear is fine, Lear's on time, Near the time, Steer it fine, Tears in eyes, Three to nine, We're aligned, Year is mine

Clock is ticking
>Got the listing, Got to wishing, Hot and sticking, Lost or missing, Plot is thickening, Pocket fishing

Close call
> Chose all, Don't stall, Low fall, Most fall, Rose tall, So small, So tall

Coast to coast
> Boast the most, Choke the rope, Don't revoke, Flows the most, Hope to choke, Knows the most, Soaked in coke, Toast to hope

Cold as ice
> Cold tonight, Hold the mic, Oh that's nice, Sold the right, Told to write

Come back
> Front back, Lunch wag<u>on</u>, One rap, Run back, Run that, Stunned that, Ton stack, Unwrap, Won that

Common knowledge
> Call for solace, Call the shot with, Long acknowledged, Lost the wallet, Not as solid, Off to college, Song is solid, Stop or stall it

Commonplace
> Dawn awaits, Dawn of days, Got erased, Longer days, On a face, On the face, Song is played, Spot and chase, What a waste

Complicated
> All are rated, Alternated, Constipated, Got inflated, Long awaited, Oscillated, Ultimatum

Compose the verse
> And blow up earth, I chose the first, Then close the hearse, Then close the search, Then throw a curve

Concerned with
> Deserted, Discerned it, I've earned it, Returned it, The first trick, The verse rips, To burst it, Unearthed it

Constant contact

Got back on track, Gone so long that, Got the bomb back, On the contract, Song is on track, Stop the combat, Want them all back

Cough it up

Awesome huh, Cause a cut, Cause a rush, Caused enough, Chopped and cut, Cost a buck, Got it stuck, Lost enough, Toss it up

Countdown

Bow down, Count now, Downtown, Found out, Loud sound, Out now, Shout out, Sound out

Court of law

For them all, Hold the ball, More in awe, Sort of raw

Courtside

Courts tried, Fortnight, Fourth try, More pride, Short ride, Short slide, Stork bite, Swordfight, Torch light

Cover up

Buckle up, Buttercup, Butter up, Cut it up, Love is what, Tougher luck

Crack addict

Act at it, Asthmatic, Back attic, Backtrack it, Bad spastic, Laugh at it, Pragmatic, Rap tactic, That drastic, That's added

Crack the whip

Back a bit, Battle it, Last a bit, Rap and spit, Slash and rip, Stack the chips, Tackle it, That commit, That's a myth

Cradle to the grave

Ages turn to days, Crazy in the ways, Daze them with a glaze, Make them do the wave, Make them say my name, Make them turn the page, Place them in a craze, Raving in a rage

Crash and burn
Cash to earn, Last to learn, Pass the germs, Passed the turn, That is stern

Credit card
Get a star, Get it hard, Get it start<u>ed</u>, Metal jar, Met the par, Never far, Pedal hard, Rent a car, Set the bar

Cross the line
Cost a dime, Lost the time, Off the rhyme, On the mind

Cry about it
I'm surrounded, Lie about it, Sight is clouded, Try to shout it, Try without it

Curtain call
Curse them all, Curve the ball, First to fall, Search the hall, Turn and fall, Verse and all, Worth it all

Curve ball
Burnt all, Cursed all, First fall, Hurt jaw, Third call, Worse call

Cut it down
Butting out, Duck around, Huddle round, Lucky sound, Underground, Up and down, Upper town, Was around, What a town

Cut it in half
Come up with cash, Hustle the cash, Hustling fast, Struck in the blast, Stuck in the past, Toughen up fast, Was it a blast

Cut it short
Lust for more, Must abort, Must retort, Rush the fort, Trust the force, Up and forth

Danger zone
>Change the flow, Change your tone, Gave a bone, Later homes, Make a clone, Take the throne, Taking home, Trace the phone

Dark as night
>Archetype, Aren't we right, Charter flight, Hard to bite, Hard to fight, Hard to write, Heart of ice, Spark the light, Starry night, Startled fright, Start to write

Dark cloud
>Bark loud, Car pound, Charts now, Dark out, Dart round, Far now, Hard sound, Harp sound, Nark's shout, Sharks out

Day by day
>Ace of bass, Ain't okay, Ate away, Crazy ay, Hate to say, Late today, Lay away, Make the pay, Make the play, Paid today, Play the game, Say my name, Stay away, Take the bait

Defeat the purpose
>A treat to flirt with, Believe the curses, Beneath the surface, Reheat the furnace, Release the circus, The beat and verses, The beat is worthless

Dead end
>Betting, Bread and, Get in, Lead in, Lead pen, Less than, Peasant, Shredded, Wedding

Dead or alive
Best on the rise, Bet on my life, Get in the eyes, Get in the side, Left it to die, Less than a nine, Pleasant and nice, West on the side

Deal with it
Feel the whip, Heal a bit, Kneel or sit, Seal the lip, Squeal a bit, Steal a bit, Wheels'll rip

Death wish
Chest hit, Guest list, Left fist, Left it, Message, Messed with, Rested, Tested

Declare war
A hail storm, An air horn, Despair for, I'm there for, Repair store, The airport, The bare core, The bear roar, To care for, To spare more

Deep freeze
Eat cheese, Heat breeze, Keep these, Please tease, Release, Speedy, Teepees, These keys, Three G's

Defend it
Amend it, A pen did, Attended, Demented, It blended, Lamented, Pretended, Rescinded, Resend it

Demo tape
Cello plays, Cello tape, Emanate, Emulate, Fellow mate, Get an A, Hello wait, Levitate, Mellow day, Sell a tape

Deny the truth
Bite the tooth, Decide to use, It might be loose, Respite and truce, So try the juice, Tie the noose, To hide the bruise, To pry it loose

Desert heat
Better seats, Debt to beat, Get to eat, Head to east, Less than cheap, Level

street, Red and deep, Test the beat,
West to east
Despite the fact
Decide to rap, From white to black, It
might react, Recite it back, Reside in
back, The ice is packed
Diamond in the rough
Might've had enough, Riding on the bus,
Silent as a hush, Tie it to a bus,
Trying to be tough, Violent to be
tough, Why does it get tough, Why you
got to cuss
Dime a dozen
Like a cousin, Like it doesn't, Night
for clubbing, Why it wasn't
Dirt off your shoulder
Birth of a culture, Earth is a boulder,
Hurling a boulder, Search in the
folder, Work like a soldier, Worse when
it's colder
Dirty tricks
Burning rift, Thirty hits, Worth a bit
Disagree
History, In a tree, In the street,
Misery, Mystery, With a beat
Disappear
Inching near, Listen clear, Listen
here, Miss the Lear, Reappear, Slinking
near, With a sneer, With a tear, With
the fear, With the peers
D.J.
Cheap way, Freeway, Heat wave, Keep
saying, Lead way, Three days, We play
Dog off its leash
Acknowledge defeat, All you can eat,
Ball in the streets, Call it for keeps,
Fall to defeat, Fall to your feet,
Knowledge is free

Dollar bill
    All until, Block and fill, Call it ill,
    Got a mill., Got a nil, On the pill
Don't worry
    Hopefully, No hurry, So furry, So
    slurry, Won't scurry
Do or die
    Bluer sky, Lose an eye, Stupid lie, Sue
    a guy, To defy, To deny, True or lie,
    Who and why, You and I
Do some time
    Choose to rhyme, Doing fine, Lose the
    mind, Newer rhyme, New to shine,
    Through a mine, To align, Two for mine,
    Use a line, You will find
Double the trouble
    Brother to brother, Cover another,
    Cover the shutters, Stumble and
    stutter, Subtle rebuttal, Under the
    rubble
Double up
    Bubble butt, Bubble up, But the luck,
    Cuddle up, Huddle up, Luck is up,
    Struggle but
Down town
    Bound down, Bow down, Count now,
    Downtown, Found out, Loud sound, Out
    now, Shout out, Sound out, Wound down
Downward spiral
    Bound denial, Crowd for miles, Found
    the file, Found the title, Round the
    fire, Sound is viral
Drop the coupe
    Bought the suit, Drop the chute, Got
    intuit, Got the loot, Got the truth,
    Hot or cute, Stop to shoot
Drop the top
    Block to block, Dot to dot, Got to
    stop, Hop and bop, Pop the lock, Stop

and drop, Stop the clock, Stop the
clot, Stop the plot

Drown the noise

Found a choice, Found a ploy, Frowns
and joys, Now rejoice, Round the boys,
Sound a voice, Sound is pois<u>on</u>

Drum and bass

Come and play, Hunger days, Months and
days, Some will say, Summer craze, Sun
and rays, Tons of ways, Thunder plays,
Thunder rains, Underage

Dusk to dawn

Hush and calm, Tough and brawn,
Underarm

Dust to dust

Cuts the rust, Hush and shush, Just
enough, Justice must, Scuff and cut,
Tough to trust

Each other
Be brothers, Be rougher, Be tougher, Breach cover, Feet shuffle, Keep double, Keep suffer<u>ing</u>, Reach under, Recover, Sleek cover, Speak utter, Speech stuttered

Earn the right
Burn the mic, Burn tonight, Hers and mine, Learn to write, Search and find, Surge of light, Turn the light, Turn the mic, Verse to write

East to west
Be the guest, Clean the mess, Deeper breath, Eat the rest, Feeling blessed, Piece of flesh, See the rest, Teach the best, We the best

Echo
Bet low, Gecko, Get go, Let go, Metro, Retro, Set go, Techno

Eight ball
Break falls, Break walls, Fate calls, Fate shall, Late call, Make small, Take all, Take calls, They fall

Eight bars
Brake hard, Date stars, Day stars, Make par, Play cards, Pray hard, Play larks, Race cars, Stay far, Stay hard

Electric shock
Detected wrong, Detectives caught, Ejection spot, It's just hip hop, Select the spot, The best hip hop, The best will drop, Dissect the song

Eleventh hour
A septic shower, Electric shower, Objective power, The heavens power, The rest is ours

Emergency room
A surge and a boom, A verse and tune, Emerge from the dune, Emerge from the gloom, In surgery soon, Is earning the boon, Is turning the room, It's worse to assume, Returning to goon

Empty handed
Betting chances, Have to stand it, Just be candid, Lets demand it, Plenty chances, Reprimanded, Steady handed, Sweaty and sick, Sweaty handed

Energy surge
Better disperse, Better than first, Enemies search, Every first, Have a rebirth, Have to rehearse, Hell is a curse, Set in reverse

Entertainment
Better rated, Better take it, Federated, Get elated, Get it tainted, Get sedated, Getting rated, Heavy ain't it, Let it rain in, Separated

Evil mind
Be aligned, Be on time, Feel the rhyme, Keep behind, Read the sign, See the line, She's a dime, She's a nine

Explain that
And lay flat, Is trained at, Then stay back, The pain's back, The rain's back, The same as, The train track, To claim that

Explicit content
Elicit context, Solicit context, Terrific contest, Terrific context, Terrific song texts, To finish contests, To mimic contexts

Eye for an eye

Climbing up high<u>er</u>, High as the sky, Sigh a goodbye, Sign on the line, Slide to the right, Tied to a lie, Try to deny, Try to rely, Why do we die

Eye to eye

Climbing high, Cry a sigh, Mighty high, Try to lie, Try to write, Why deny, Why rely

Face the truth
> Break a tooth, Break it loose, Hate to choose, Hate to lose, Play for you, Play the flute, Waste the use

Face the music
> Hate to use it, Make amusing, Make a new hit, Making you sick, Say what you think, Take or lose it, They abuse it, They could use it

Fade away
> Aces played, Chase away, Great array, Made the day, Making way, Paid to say, Pay to play, Play to play, Rain today

Fade out
> Laid out, Lay down, May doubt, Played out, Play loud, Say loud, Steak out, They doubt, They shout

Fail to see
> A to Z, Ail and scream, Make a plea, Make them see, Pale and weak, Wail and weep, Way to be

Fame and fortune
> Blame the culture, Came with forces, Days a scorcher, Hate the vultures, Same as torture, Take the torture, Wake the morning

Fasten the seatbelt
> Bash as the beat melts, Flashes of heat felt, Laugh when they scream help, Scrapping what he dealt, Trashing what we sell

Fast lane
Abstain, Act sane, Back pain, Bad day, Cash came, Cash game, Cast shame, Glass pane, Last came, That pain, That's fame

Fast zone
Backbone, Back home, Bad clone, Bad jones, Bad loan, Calzone, Cast stones, Last known

F.B.I.
Best to buy, Best to try, Get behind, Get me high, Get tonight, Guess we lie, Just deny, Let it fly, Messy guy

F.C.C.
Blessed to be, Guess with me, Guest M.C., Lesson three, Let me be, Let me see, Mess with me, Press is free, S.T.D., Test the seas

Fear nothing
Hear cussing, Hear something, Near crushing, Tears running, Tears rushing, We're coming

Feature presentation
Creature of temptation, Deeper laceration, Keep me from temptation, Keep the conversation, Peace among the nation, Peaceful revelation, Teacher of the nation, Teaching to be patient

Feedback
Beat that, Be stacked, Cheat at, Deep track, Heat that, Lead at, Meat sack, Meet at, Peek at, Read that, See that

Feed the track
Be attached, Evil's back, Free to rap, G is back, Lead the pack, Meet the pack, People rap, Read the back

Feed the verse
Be from birth, Be the first, Bleeding hurts, Feel the worst, Need to curse,

Speak in turn, Speech is slurred, Treat them worse

Feel the beat

Cease the peace, Feed the beast, Heal the street, Keep it neat, Knees to feet, Meal for free, Need to eat, See defeat, Steal the heat, Steal the keys, We retreat

Fever rises

Beat surprises, Be decisive, Be the nicest, Demonizes, Keep it rising, Keep the license, Legalize it, Need disguises, Peace arises, See horizons

Fiber optics

Hide and lock it, Nice to talk with, Pry the pockets, Ride or rock it, Try to block it, Try to cop it

Fifth element

Listen again, Mix in a blend, Pitching a tent, Risk detriment, Stick in cement, This elegant, This evident, This is the end, This testament, With evidence, With sentiment

Fight back

Buy that, Ice pack, Like that, Nightcap, Fight that, Ride that, Right track, Tight track, Type that, Wide gap, Write raps, Write that

Fight fair

Eyes stare, I dare, I swear, Light air, Light hair, Might tear, Night air, Nightmare, Right there, Why care

Figure of speech

Eager to reach, Isn't deceit, Jingle the keys, Pick up the beat, Pick up the street, Shivered and weak, Sit on the beach, This is a treat

Fill up the glass
Listen to rap, Little of that, River of cash, Spit on the ash, Still in the cast, This is the wrath

Fine line
Blind rhyme, Buy time, Dry eyes, Fly by, High time, I shine, Mind mine, Night sky, Nine times, Rhymes shine

Fingertips
In a split, Inner wish, Inner wit, Little bit, Mingle with, Single bit, Sinners trip, Thinner lips, Tinker with

Fire burns
I return, Rhymes immersed, Tired nerves, Try reverse, Try to learn, While it turns

First class
Burn trash, Burst past, Cursed that, Hearse passed, Hurts bad, Nurse fast, Thirst passed, Worst trash

First place
Birth place, Third case, Turned bass, Verse aced, Worse face, Worst case

Flashback
Blast at, Fast track, Gasp at, Grasp that, Lack that, Last track, Nab that, Pass back, Passed that, That's rap, That's that

Flesh and blood
Best above, Fresh as mud, Get a hug, Just a shove, Just for love, Let it flood, Test the drug

Flip the phone
Drip and foam, Rip the chrome, Sit and moan, Sit at home, Trips to Rome

Flip the script
Bit my lip, Fit to spit, Listen quick, Lit the wick, Rip a lip, Spit the

tricks, This is it, With the click, With the tricks

Foaming at the mouth

Chose to be about, Closing up and out, Focusing without, Home is at the house, Knowing all about, Know what it's about, Showing up without, Show'll go all out, Those are peeking out, Those'll creep around, Throw it out the house

Focus on the task

Close enough to pass, Hope it's not the last, Joke is just a laugh, Poke it in the ass

Follow the line

Offer some time, Sorrow is mine, Start to unwind, Stop on a dime, Thought it was mine

Follow the words

Hollow the earth, Sorrow and hurt, Stall on the verse, Swallow the verse, Swallow the worst

Food for thought

Choose to drop, Chose to stop, Do to stop, Lose a lot, Lose the spot, Mood is blocked, Shoes and socks

Force of habit

Coarse and spastic, Corner attic, Course to track it, Forth and back in, For the addict

Forgive and forget

The fifth from the left, To give than to get, To live and to let

For the fame

Bored of change, Born the name, More ashamed, Order came, Order rain, Or the name, Pour the rain, Shorter chain, Sort of lame

For the money
> More than nutty, Pour the honey, Sort of funny, Sort of runny, Told the dummy

For the people
> Before the prequel, Cold and evil, Hold the weasel, More than lethal, Or an equal, Sold a sequel

Four of a kind
> Border the line, Coarse in the rhyme, Force in the mind, Hold up a sign, More to unwind, Older than nine, Sold for a dime

Free my mind
> Be defined, Keeping time, Need to find, Peace of mind, See the line, We decide, We define

Freestyle battle
> Beat the paddle, Leak my bladder, She might tattle, Street side chatter, Street style rapper

Freeze over
> Be sober, Cheap poser, Creep closer, Four leaf clover, Street chosen, Street roamer

Freight train
> Change lanes, Make gain, Make rain, Make way, Place blame, Play game, Stay sane, Take names, Take pain

Fresh air
> Best pair, Chest hair, Get there, Get where, Just stare, Less care, Less fair

Friday
> Highway, Might say, My way, Sideways

Front of the line
> Come up behind, Cover the sign, Money is time, Running to hide, Struggle to find, Struggle to rhyme, Summer to shine, Thundering rhyme

Front page

Come play, Drums play, Drunk craze,
Hunt game, One day, Some craze, Some
day, Some phase, Sunday, Untraced

Fundamental

Comes torrential, Run the pencil, Some
are mental, Under tension

Funny bone

But alone, Coming home, Cut the tone,
Dummy clone, Money prone

Future's bleak

Chew the piece, Chose the beat, Do for
weeks, Losing streak, Move the streets,
Truce to peace, Truth is weak, Two for
three

Gag reflex

Ask respect, Badly wrecked, Magic jests, Raps defect, Rap secrets, That reflects, That rejects

Gamble it away

Chances are okay, Damaging the brain, Handle it today, Hand'll hit your face, Land a little late, Rambling all day, Ran a different way, Tangle in a maze

Game on

Blame on, Day's dawn, Made wrong, Play on, Same song, Stay long, Wait on, Way gone

Game plan

Blade fan, Main land, Played hand, Same fan, Say can, Shame can, Spray can

Game point

Great choice, Main boys, Same joint, Same voice, Spray poison

Garter belt

Caramel, Far to hell, Heart has felt, Smart to tell, Start to sell, Start to smell, Start to swell

Gas mask

Blast at, Fast cash, Fast track, Gasp at, Grasp that, Lack that, Last track, Laugh at, Nab that, Pass back, Passed that, Pass that, That's rap, That's that

Get the cash
Bet on that, Jet'll crash, Let it pass, Leveled flat, Mess with that, Pet the cats, Settle back, Set to smash

Ghost writer
Blow fire, Flow's tighter, Flow's viral, Glows brighter, Go higher, Known fighter, Most vital, No liar, Show fighter, Throw spiral

Giraffe neck
A bad check, Elastic, Fantastic, In bad debt, In plastic, It's half empty, The cash left, The last left, The last stretch

Give me the mic
Glistening bright, Grip on it tight, Into the light, Is it tonight, Isn't it right, Is to recite, Living a life, Living tonight

Glitch in the system
Finish the mission, Hit the ignition, In the position, Into submission, It is a mission, Listen in with them, Listen to wisdom

Glove compartment
Blood'll darken, Flood the market, Love to sharpen, Stud department, What apartment

Glue stick
Abused it, Amused with, Blew spit, Eluded, Lose it, Music, Slewed in, Through with, Use it, You sit

Go after him
Flow mastering, No aspirin, So happening

Gold mine
Bold line, Cold spine, Hold signs, Old time, Sold nine, Told time

Good news

A deuce, Could bruise, Could lose, Good shoes, Look dude, Should use, To lose, Wood shoes, Would choose

Good or bad

Could react, Looking at, Should attract, Stood and rapped, Stood intact, Withstood the fact, Wood in back

Got the blues

A lot to lose, Cockatoos, Cops abuse, Got one too, Hotter view, Lost a shoe, Not a few, Rotten juice, Spot the clues, Stopped and threw, Stop the news

Got the time

Drop a line, Got combined, Hottest rhyme, Not divine, Not refined, Stop decline, Stopping sign, Stopping time, Stop the rhyme

Grain of sand

Changing hands, Gave a chance, Gave a glance, Made enhanced, Make a man, Pay advance, Stay entranced, Take a stand, Wait to land

Greedy eyes

Be despised, Be the wise, Free to try, Greasy fries, Need supplies, Screaming cries, See me fly, See me try, Speedy lines

Grit my teeth

Admit defeat, Grip the seat, Hit delete, Hit the streets, Isn't sweet, It's discrete, Spit to beats, Trick or treat

G spot

Beat's hot, Be hot, Cheap talk, See not, See spots, Treetop, We got

G star

Be hard, Be part, Cheap car, Regard, See far, See stars, Sleep hard, We are

Guide the way

Cried today, File away, Hide away, Like to say, Mile a day, Pried away, Ride the wave, Shine the ray, Try to stay

Gym class

Grim past, Pinned back, Sing that, Slim fast, Spill that, Swim fast, Syntax, Think back, Think fast, Wind blast, Win fast

Hair raising
Air's fading, Chairs facing, Race chasing, Rare phrasing, Swears blazing, Their craving, They dared me, They're crazy, They're staring

Hall of fame
Ball's in play, Call the game, Crawl in pain, On the name, Tall and plain, Wall of shame

Hallucinate
Abusive state, Accumulate, Adjudicate, A lucid state, Amuse the nation, A putrid fate, Assume the fate, I choose to hate, Illuminate, To rule the great

Hallway walls
All day long, All dissolved, All in all, All involved, All the balls, Call the calls, Caught the fall

Halogen lamp
Abdomen cramp, As an advance, Battle the clan, Practice the dance, Saddle up man, Sat in the stands

Halt and stop
Call the cops, Call the shots, Fall and drop, Halter top, Hard and soft, Parking lot

Hammer and nail it
Angered and hated, Chances are fading, Glamorous ain't it, Handle the pain with, Hang it and frame it, Land of the famous, Manage to fail it, Slander, Stamp it and mail it

Handcuffed

And huff, And puff, Bland stuff, Can't bluff, Can't cuss, Man up, Sand's rough, Slammed shut, Stand tough, Stand up

Handle it

And a bit, Cancel it, Candle lit, Dance a bit, Dance with it, Handle this, Plan to rip, Ran with it, Stand a bit, Stand or sit, Tangled with

Handstand

And and, And prance, Band fans, Banned land, Can-can, Can dance, Can't answer, Grand land, Sandman, Stranded

Hands tied

Can't hide, Dance wild, Demand rights, Landslide, Pan fried, Plans died, Ran wild, Stand lies, Transpired

Hard knock life

Are chalk-white, Hard knots tied, Hardtop ride, Smarts talk wise, Star shot sky, Star spotlight

Hard of hearing

All are cheering, Are appearing, Art careering, Car is steering, Guards are nearing, Songs are searing, Start appealing, Start appearing

Hard time

All mine, All rhymes, Call sign, Charred rhyme, Small crime, Smalltime, Star sign

Hard to accept

Heart in the chest, Part of the rest, Smart and adept, Smart as the rest, Start to detest, Start with a guess

H.D.T.V.

Hate this really, Make a C.D., May be greedy, Take me freely, Take the G.T., Wait to see me

Head to head

Dead ahead, Get the bread, Get to bed, Pens and lead, Said instead, Send the Feds, Shred the lead

Health hazard

Best batter, Sell faster, Spell master

Hear it out

Cheer about, Cheer and shout, Fear about, Here to doubt, Jeer about, Jeer and shout, Rear around, Near to doubt, Year of drought

Heart attack

Artifact, Cardiac, Farther back, Hard to rap, Pardon that, Smarts and knacks, Starter cap, Starter pack, Start to rap

Heart of a lion

Sorry for trying, Start with the crying, Stop with the lying

Heart of gold

Common cold, Hard and cold, Hot or cold, Hot to hold, Part of old, Start to fold

Heart rate

Car brakes, Guard gate, Partake, Start late, Start straight

Heat up the track

Creep up in back, Deeper than that, Eagles attack, Neat in a stack, People that rap, Seats in the back, Speed up the rap, Street rap is back, Sweeter than that

Heat wave

Beat plays, Be brave, Behave, Be saved, Depraved, Feet stay, Free stay, He say she say, Leeway, Neat way, Speed chase

Heaven or hell

Bet it'll sell, Fell in the well, Head isn't well, Seven to tell, Smelled it and fell, Telling it well, Well it'll sell

Heavy weight

Already late, Any fate, Any rate, Any state, Emanate, Escalate, Federate, Get it late, Many wait, Petty fate, Steady rate, When's the date

High light

By night, Eyesight, Fly by, Hindsight, I might, Limelight, Shine bright, Side by, Sideline, Twilight, Why fight, Write tight

High noon

By moonlight, High dunes, Like soon, Try two, Typhoon, Write tunes

High pressure

Dimension, Like lectures, My sector, Nice texture, Side venture, Try nectar, Why mention

High speed chase

Dicey ways, High heat wave, Light speed craze, Light speed daze, Likely fades, Right beat plays, Wide leeway

High stakes

Blind dates, By day, Crime rates, Dilates, Find ways, Fine days, Gyrate, Highways, Line breaks, Mind plays, Rhyme breaks, Rhyme play, Sign states, Violates, Why wait

Highway

Blind date, By day, Crime rate, Fine day, High stakes, I say, Mind play, My way, Rhyme play, Signs say, Violate

Hip hop

Click clock, Criss cross, Flip flop, Hit stop, Lip locked, Pit stop, Thick socks, This clock, This stops, Which spot, With cops

Hip hop is dead
> Criss cross the lead, Flip flopping headfirst, Get off the bed, It's not the meds, Just chop and shred, Lips locked and said, Sing songs instead

Hip hop revival
> Get caught and violated, The top disciple, This song is viral, This spot is vital, This stops denial

Hit rewind
> Fit the crime, Gift for rhyme, It's the time, Just unwind, Lift it high, Listen why, Sit and dine, Spit and rhyme

Hold my breath
> Cold as death, Cold as hell, Gold and treasure, Golden chest, Gold is left, Sold the rest, Stole what's left, Swords and vests, Told to guess

Hollow out
> All about, Called about, Call and shout, Follow round, Sorrow now, Swallow loud, Swallow proud, Tomorrow's now

Hollywood
> Are we good, Heart of wood, Jolly good, Sorry could, Sorry should, Sorry would

Hometown
> Grossed out, Gross sound, Hopes found, Low ground, No sound, Shown round, So loud, Throw down, Toes down

Honestly
> Apology, Audibly, Bother me, Got for free, Modestly, Shoddily, Wobbly

Hospital patient
> Got a replacement, Obstacles facing, Possible placement, Shocked in amazement, Tossed in the basement

Hot box

Bought stocks, Cop shots, Got shocks, Knocked off, Not talk, Pop rocks, Top shots

Hunt down

Drums pound, Dumb sound, Fun sound, Jump out, Numb now, One pound, Run round, Some sound, Some town, Stunt round, Uptown

Hustle the beat

Brush up the fleet, Bustling street, Flush and defeat, Hush up and speak, Hush up the street, Muscles are weak, Shuffle the feet, Subtle and sleek

Hydraulics

Bite on it, I called it, Like college, Like comics, Right logic, Write honest, Write solid

Hydrochloric acid

Eyes are sore and plastic, Ice into the glasses, I support assassins, Might absorb the flashes, Might contort the spastic, Tight control is drastic, Why report the lashes, Write to bore the masses

Hype man

Flight lands, Like fans, Mic stand, Night plans, Right hand, White sand

Hyperventilate

Fires detonate, Fly and get away, Hype'll set it straight, Time to meditate, Try to set it straight

Ice cold

Lies told, Like old, Mics old, Might hold, Right's sold, White gold

Ice pack

Buy that, Fight back, Fight that, Like that, Nightcap, Ride that, Right track, Tight track, Type that, Wide gap, Write raps, Write that

Ignite the fire

Delightful smile, Incite a riot, Inside the wire, Is gliding higher, Provide attire, The light's acquired, The right desire

Ill rhymes

Fill time, Kill time, Nil times, Skills shine, Skintight, Spill mine, Still fine, Thick slime, This time, Twin lines, Will sign

Immediate action

A speedy reaction, Is feeling the traction, Misleading distraction, Receiving a fraction, The key is attraction, To need satisfaction

Immense pressure

Defense gesture, Intense measures, Intense tension, The best treasure, The rest's censored, To sense pleasure

Immortal

A boulder, A moral, Amoral, Disorder, Immoral, It's colder, It's older, The border, The portal, The shoulder, To quarrel

Immune to the fact
A room in the back, As soon as it's back, Assume this or that, At noon in the back, A tune in the track, A wound in the back, The glue will attract

Important to know
An orphan at home, Discordant and slow, Disorder will grow, Distorting the show, Retort with the flow, Support at the show

Impossible
An obstacle, A popsicle, Illogical, It's optical, It's possible, The hospital

Improvement
A student, Be prudent, Conclusion, Delusion, Diffuse it, Illusion, The movement

In a minute
Finish in it, Intermittent, Is a menace, Is diminished, It's infinite, It's within it

In conclusion
An illusion, An infusion, An intrusion, In delusion, It's amusing, With allusion

Inconsistent
In submission, Insufficient, Intermission, Intermittent, In the distance, It's a mission, Need assistance, With persistence

Increase the sound
And be surrounded, Indecent shout, Police the crowd, Release the hounds, The heat and drought, The streets are found, This beat's profound, To speak about

Indecent

Diseases, Displeases, Impeding, Increasing, In pieces, In season, It freezes, It pleases, It's recent, With reason

Ineffective

A detective, Be a skeptic, It is hectic, It is septic, It's dissected, It's elective, It's electric

Inexplicable

It gets critical, It gets literal, It gets mystical, It gets physical, It's elliptical

Infinity

Affinity, Divinity, In misery, It's history, This mystery, Vicinity, With liberty

Ink in the pen

Blink in the end, Drink with a friend, In the defense, Into the bend, Think and pretend, Think it again, Think it's the end

In most cases

In low places, In those places, Then showcase it, The slow races, With ghost faces, With no traces

In or out

In a drought, Sing and shout, Think about, With a doubt

Instrumental

In the rental, In the temple, Singing gentle, With parental

Insult

A cult, Adult, A jolt, And sulk, Result

Intelligence

Benevolent, Irrelevant, Is relevant, Its redolent, This element, With elegance

Interstate
A sinner pays, Enervate, Eviscerate, Immigrate, Incinerate, Is it fate, Isn't great, Win the chase, With this rate

In the hood
Built of wood, It withstood, Wish I could, Wish it would, With the goods

In the club
In the dust, In the mud, Isn't just, Link it up, With a thrust, With the trust

Introduction
It's corruption, Reproduction, Sick eruption, Spit reduction, This deduction, This production, This seduction, With a suction

Ipecac
Bit of that, Fill a track, Give it back, Isn't whack, Kick it back, Spit it back, This or that

Itch to scratch
Listen fast, Spit the facts, Spit the raps, This or that, Whip a batch, With the fact

Jacob watch

Ache and throb, Break the lock, Chase the block, Hate the boss, Laser shot, Take a loss, Take a walk, Take it off, Wade across

Jack of all trades

Back in a day, Back on my way, Half of a day, Plaques on the way, Rap in your face, Slacking all day, That is okay, Trash in the way

Jack hammer

Back panel, Bad anger, Bad angle, Bad gamble, Bad manners, Last channel, Rap vandal, That manner, Track strangled

Jack in the box

Back at the top, Battle the clock, Blast and get knocked, Fast as a fox, Last at the top, Master the block, That will unlock, Travel the block

Jaws of life

Drop a line, Fought for life, Gnaw and bite, Got a strike, Laws and rights, Lost the right, Lots of pride, Not polite, Ostracize, Raw but tight

Jazz music

Last to sit, Pass through it, Rap grew quick, That's soothing

Jealousy

Destiny, Enemy, Felony, Heavily, Melody, Messily, Remedy, Steadily

Jewelry store
  Cruelly told, Duel with swords, News report, Through the door, Truth be told, You report
Job to do
  All but two, Got me dude, Got to you, Hopping through, Mob the crew, Rockets flew, Sorry dude, Talk to you, Walk in shoes
Joke around
  Boast about, Closer now, Go to town, Lower ground, Mow it down, Nope not now, No surround, Overthrow the crown
Join the club
  Boy it's tough, Choice is what, Hoist it up, Point it up
Judge and jury
  Budge the ruling, Drugs and jewelry, Grudge with fury, Sludge is pouring, Touches truly, Tough and grueling
Judges orders
  Budge a shoulder, Bust the border, Dust the shoulder, Hustle corners, Rough and colder, Such disorder, Suffer for them
Juggle at once
  Double the stunts, Muscle and brunt, Struggle and stunt, Subtle and cunning
Juggle at the same time
  Come up with a fake smile, Double up insane rhymes, Muddle and mistake lines, Puddles when the rain dries, Running for the state line, Struggle to create rhymes
Jump around
  Bump the sound, Dump it down, Dump it out, Sunk it down, Underground, Wonder now

Jump up and down
   Become dumber now, Come up from town, From underground, Got busted down, Some wonder now

Jump off
   Become boss, Dumb thought, Gunshot, Some cost, Sung soft, Sun's hot, Tongue caught, Uncross, Upshot

Jump start
   Come far, Dumb part, Fun part, One chart, Some are, Stunt car

Justified
   Bust an eye, Electrified, Festive night, Gets it right, Get the ride, Pesticide, Rectified, Testified

Just in time
   Bust a line, Bust a rhyme, Crush the rhyme, Fuss and whine, Hush the rhyme, Lust's desire, Must rewind, Rush the line

Just like me
   Best I be, Dress nice please, Fresh like me, Gets dicey, Less slightly

Juvenile delinquent
   Choose the rhyme with intent, You can find an instant

Kamikaze
>   Call the posse, Fought the army, Gaunt
>   and scrawny, Got the body, Got them off
>   me, Hot as coffee, Not as sloppy

Kerosene
>   Air is clean, Bare and seen, Caribbean,
>   Dare to dream, Fair but mean, Have a
>   dream, Share a dream

Keep it coming
>   Beat is humming, Be discussing, Cheat
>   and bluffing, Feet are running, Leave
>   with nothing

Keep it up
>   Beat the luck, Deeper rut, Eat the
>   glut, Heap of junk, Seal it shut,
>   Street is tough

Keep my head up
>   People fed up, Secret weapon, We were
>   set up

Keep the peace
>   Beat's released, Beat to pieces, Eat
>   the feast, Feat's defeated, Heat
>   release, Meet the beast, Reap the
>   least, Unleash the beast

Keep trying
>   Freestyling, Heat's firing, He's lying,
>   Retiring, Retry it, She's lying,
>   Street's crying, Weak rhyming

Keyboard
>   Be torn, Deep roar, Free form, Keep
>   more, Keep score, Knee sore, Record,
>   Restored, Reward, Seashore

Kick back
      Blink fast, Click clack, List that,
      Mismatch, Miss that, Quick rap, Sick
      rap, Sink fast, Think fast, Think that,
      With rap

Kick dirt in the face
      Its hurting the case, Just working to
      make, Slip words into place, Win first
      in the race

Kick down the door
      In town to score, Rip out and pour, Rip
      out the thorns, Whipped out of form,
      With sound that roars

Kick it off
      Bit it off, Lick it off, Nickel toss,
      Sick and cough<u>ing</u>, Sip a coff<u>ee</u>, With a
      pop

Kick the dust off
      In the bus stop, Quit the gunshots,
      Quit the tough talk, This just must
      stop

Kilo to kilo
      Below the zero, Be no amigo, Hero to
      zero, Zero to hero

Kind of bad
      <u>A</u>lign the track, <u>B</u>eside the fact, Blind
      as bats, Eyes in back, Find the rat,
      Hide in back, Might attack, Rhyme and
      rap, Time to act

King is back
      Bring it back, Drink to that, Figure
      that, In a flash, It's a fact, Riddle
      that, Sing or rap, Sprinkle that, Think
      it's bad, Think of that

King size
      Blink eyes, Blink twice, Disguise, Pink
      eye, Sick eyes, Six tries, Switch
      sides, Think why

Kiss goodbye
Bliss is nice, It's alright, Listen why, Mystify, Sit and try, This is dry, This is nice, This is why, Whisper lies

Kneecap
Beat that, Feedback, Free rap, Lead back, Leap at, Meet at, Relapse, See that, Street cat, Street rap

Knee high stockings
Beats are knocking, Feel like talking, Freestyle talking, Seaside walking, See eyes gawking, Street side walking, We try rocking

Knock it off
Block is hot, Block the shot, Drop the top, Got too soft, Lost the spot, Not the top, Pause to stop, Spot the top, Walk the talk

Know how
Flow now, Go round, Low down, No sound, Oh wow, So loud, So now, So proud, Toe down

Know it all
Blow the call, Overall, Owe it all, So in awe, Throw the ball, Won't recall

Label deal
> Ate a meal, Break the seal, Made of steel, May appeal, May reveal, Play the field, Same appeal, They conceal

Lab rat
> Bad at, Blast at, Fast track, Flashback, Gasp at, Grasp that, Lack that, Last track, Nab that, Pass back, Passed that, Sat back, That's rap, That's that

Lace the track
> Erase the fact, Play it back, Trace it back, Waste of that

Lakeside
> Bass line, Great rhyme, Hate crimes, Lakeside, Make signs, Race line, State line, Statewide, Take mine, Taste fine

Landslide
> Can't find, Can't hide, Can try, Chance might, Dance right, Hands tied, Mankind, Pants high, Stand high, Stand lies

Larger than life
> Art of a spy, Charter a flight, Hard as goodbyes, Hard on the rise, Smarter and wiser, Start it up right

Last chance
> Backhand, Bad bands, Fat man, Flat lands, Hat stand, Last dance, Tap dance, That's banned

Last night
Bad eyes, Bad side, Bad sight, Capsize, Chastise, Fast ride, Flashlight, Rap rhymes, That bright, That's tight

Laugh it up
Backing up, Pass it up, Smack it shut, That's enough, Track is cut

Launch pad
Along that, Bomb back, Compact, Contact, Contract, On track, Strong fact

Lay it out
Play and shout, Play around, Say with doubt, Say without, Way in doubt, Weigh it out

Leader of the pack
Feel it when it cracks, Heating up the track, See it in the back, Sequel to the track

Lead pencil
Bets settled, Get cancelled, Head's mental, Head tension, Spread tension

Lead the way
Be the bait, Be today, Cheaper way, Free to stay, Keep it straight, Knead the clay, Need to wait, Real estate, Recreate, Speed away, We debate

Lear jet
Clear quest, Ears wet, Fear death, Near death, Near debt, Steer west, We're dressed

Leather belt
Better help, Feather's fell, Head'll melt, Settle debts

Left-handed
Can't stand it, Enhance it, Get branded, Just landed, Left stranded, Let sand in

Left to right

Best of five, Restless night, Test the mic, Test the ride

Legal aid

Evil ways, Please behave, See today, Sequel played,

Legal limit

Beat a minute, Be so timid, Lethal minute, Need a gimmick, People mimic, See the finish

Lethal dose

Be as close, Beat the flows, Keep the post, Legal load, See the most, We supposed

Let it be

Ebony, Enemy, Felony, Heavy beat, Lesson three, Melody, Never see, Remedy, Secondly, Steadily

Liar, liar

Find a buyer, Find the wire, Fire Fire, Higher wire, I admire, I inspire

Lickety-split

Listen to it, Mission to spit, Rickety lips, Ripping it quick, Slippery rift, Stick to the script, Tickle and itch

Light it up

By the cup, Find a nut, Fire up, Guided up, Like a cut, Try with what, Write it up

Life is bad

Biting back, Like the track, Might react, Try to rap, Write the track

Life is good

Bite the wood, I withstood, Like it could, Like it should, Pry the hood

Lifelong

By dawn, Icon, Lights on, Right wrong, Tight song, Write songs

Lighter fluid
Biting through it, Lie in ruins, Like the music, Try to do it, Why ensue it

Lightning bolt
Decide to fold, Eyes behold, Icy cold, Fight the cold, Like the gold, Mic is old, Psychic told, Rights are sold, Shy but bold

Lightning strike
Find the light, Like to write, Rhyme and write, Rhyme sing write, Ride a bike

Like an addict
Delight and gladness, Hide in attics, Hype the magic, Quite dramatic, Slightly static, Strike a matchstick, Writes erratic

Like a brother
Bite the rubber, Like the other, Might discover, Night'll cover, Write another

Like to fight
Bite the mic, Climb the height, Like a knife, Nice advice, Price is right, Right to write, Slice the ice, Spike the hype

Limousine
Guillotine, In a dream, Is supreme, Isn't seen, Nicotine, Skip a scene, Strip it clean, This extreme, With a team

Lips sealed
Infield, It's real, Misdeal, Six wheels, This feel, With shields, With steel

Listen up
Dip and duck, In a rut, Rip it shut, Isn't luck, Nip and tuck, Wish it luck, With a buck, With a cut

Lock and load
> Block the road, Lost control, Lost the flow, Rock and roll, Shop and go, Walk the road

Lost and found
> Awesome sound, Chalk it out, Got around, Hop around, Not for now, Rock the sound, Stomp the ground, Talk it out

Lost the fight
> Boss tonight, Cost a life, Cross the mic, Lost the mic, Talk alike, Walk alike

Loudspeaker
> Crowd pleaser, Down deeper, Sound features, Sound seeker, Sound seizure, Town people

Love is pain
> Done with playing, Summer rain, Sun and rain, Thunder rains, Under came, Was the same, Wonders came

Lower class
> Flow is fast, Over that, Pro at that, Slow or fast, Soda gas, Throw a pass, Throw it back, Throw the trash

Loyalty
> Boil heat, Oil leak, Royalty, Spoil me

Luxury cars
> Cut in the scar, Hustle it hard, Nothing but stars, Struck in the heart, Suffering hard, Touch in the heart

Lyrics
> Dearest, Fear it, Hear it, Physics, Nearest, Near it, Spirits, Steer it

Magic number
Ashes under, Clap like thunder, Crack and thunder, <u>Fan</u>tastic wonder, <u>Ran</u>sack and plunder

Main point
Fake coin, Game point, Same choice, Same joint

Major league
Lay beneath, Play to keep, Razor deep, Take a knee, Takes a week

Make a mistake
Face is defaced, Faces to face, Lacing the bass, Pay for the date, Taking the bait

Make a move
Break it loose, Break the mood, Hate the truth, Pay the dues, Take or lose

Make a single
Break the brittle, Grated shingle, Hate the middle, Pain is ting<u>ling</u>, Pay a little, Play the fiddle, Raining tinsel

Make it happen
Break it back in, Fake and acting, Hate distractions, Shake and clapping, Take an action, Wake up laughing

Make it hot
Break a lot, Places swapped, Race the block, Take it off, Take the spot

Make it rain
Bass is cra<u>zy</u>, Bass is plain, Bass is playing, Face is plain, Take the pain, Take the plane

Make it work
> Shake the dirt, Take the hurt

Make or break
> Ace of bass, Ache and shake, Break a plate, Change the rate, Fate is fate

Make the transfer
> Change the answer, Take the chances

Man to man
> And again, Chances stand, Scan the land, Stand a chance, Stand again, Standard plan

Martial art
> A la carte, All the charts, Are apart, Fall apart, False alarm, Far apart, Hard to start, Smart and sharp, Start the car

Mastermind
> Back in time, Faster rhyme, Last to find, Pass the time, Rap and rhyme, Tap the mind

Master of ceremonies
> Faster compared to slowly, Last for a second "homie,"

Matter of fact
> After the act, Battle the track, Bladder attack, Disaster attacks, Last to react, Master of rap, Stab in the back, Tackle the rap

Maximum potential
> Acting dumb and mental, Lack the comprehension, Magic from the pencil, Rap becomes essential

Maybe not
> Behaving shocked, Gave a lot, Make it hot, Save a spot, Weighs a lot

M.C.
> Can be, Can see, Empty, Plenty, Ready, Sexy, Steady, Sweaty

Medicated
Dedicated, Desolated, Elevated, Federated, Generated, Never made it, Regulated, Separated, Serenaded, Venerated

Melting point
Felt the joy, Felt the noise, Get destroyed, Selfish choice, Selling ploys

Mental challenge
Pencil talent, Sensing saddened, Sentence scavenger, Set the cadence, Threat to balance

Mic check
Biceps, High debt, High step, High tech, Might get, Mind check, Mindset, Right left, Times get, Typeset, Write texts

Microchip
Die for it, Eyes are split, Like to spit, Right to sit, Strike the whip

Microphone
Microscope, Might disown, Like the chrome, Like to flow, Like to go, Like to know, Right to joke

Middle ages
Dissipated, Flip the pages, Liberated, Mitigated, Riddled phrases, Sick and wasted, With a razor

Middle class
Bitter past, Did the math, Little cash, Little clash, Riddle that, Sit and gasp, With a blast

Middle of the night
Fiddle with the mic, Little is alright, Sitting in the light

Mile after mile
    Hide the denial, Style's versatile,
    While it's in style, Wind up the style,
    Vile as a bile
Miles a minute
    Finest linens, Kind of timid, Mind your
    business, Smiles diminish, Style's a
    gimmick, Try to mimic, While I finish
Miles per hour
    Cries are louder, I devour, Mind is
    power, Rhymes are sour, Styles devour
Mind freeze
    Buy these, Fine breeze, Fine cheese,
    High seas, High speeds, I please, Mind
    squeeze, Mind tease, Siamese, Time
    piece
Mind over matter
    Climb up the ladder, Hyper reactor,
    Rhymes going faster, Times going
    faster, Try flowing faster
Mind power
    Buy flowers, Flight tower, Nine hours,
Try hours
Mind your business
    Crime statistics, Find what is this,
    Kind of rigid, Time in prison, Try to
    mimic
Mirror reflection
    Bigger infection, Give it protection,
    Inner deception, In the direction,
    Rigor objection, Scissor dissection
Misbehave
    Give away, Infiltrate, Instigate, It's
    a faze, It's the way, Miss the play,
    Mist and haze, Simple way, With a save
Mix a drink
    Hit or sink, In a blink, It's the
    brink, Rip the skin, Sit and think,
    With a wink, With the ink

Mix and master
>Big disaster, Bricks and plaster, Lips are faster, Skip the chapter

Mix it up
>Is it luck, Kick the dust, Miss the cup, Pixie dust, Rip it up, Spits it up

Mixmaster
>Distracted, Spit faster, Think faster

Moment of truth
>Chose an excuse, Open the booth, Over the news, Over the views, Sober abuse

Moment of time
>Don't hit rewind, Go with the times, So it reminds, So it's a crime, So it's a sign

Monday
>Come play, One day, One way, Some day, Some way, Sunday

Monkey in the middle
>Jumpy just a little, Nothing but a riddle, Something makes it twinkle

Monotony
>A mockery, Done sloppily, Monopoly, The company

More than that
>Explore the track, Ignore the fact, Form a pact, For the rap, Roar it back, Sort of cracked, Stored in back, Wore the cap

Mortal combat
>Born to bomb back, More along that, Order falls back, Sort of saw that

Mouth to mouth
>Clouds are out, Count it down, House to house, Out the house, Shout it out, Sound it out, Sounds profound, Town to town

Move out the way
Choose how to say, Cruise down the bay, Lose out today, New sound to play, Shoes found the way, True sound will pay

Must be right
Bust a rhyme, Hush it tight, Lust for life, Other night, Stuff to write, Thunder strike, Underwrite, What a sight

Mystery
Busily, History, In the street, Misery, With the beat

Name of the game
Day after day, Facing the pain, Making it rain, Playing the same, Shame to the name, Taking the fame

N.B.A.
Center page, End the day, End the game, Meant to say, Penny pays, Plenty ways, Send the rain

Necessary
Better bury, Chest is hairy, Estuary, Getting scary, Head is airy, Legendary, Military, Secretary, Sedentary

Need to know basis
Beats'll go racing, Deal me no aces, Feet and sole laces, Leave to go places, Meet and know faces, Speed the slow paces, Streets and souls chasing

Neighborhood
Break the wood, Faced and stood, Later's good, Make it good, Way it should

Neon lights
Be alright, Be on right, Cheaper price, Eon's life, Keep on writing, Read or write, See the light

Nerve gas
Cursed at, First at, Hurts that, Search pack, Turn back, Urge back

Nervous system
Learn the mission, Search the kitchen, Surge of wisdom, Urge to listen, Verbalism

Never back down
>Get it back now, Get to act out, Level at now, Sever that sound

Never forget
>Have to neglect, Letters are set, Never regret, Settle the bet, Settle the debt

Never stop
>Better spot, Ever drop, Feathers drop, Get the top, Kettle's hot, Mega hot, Second spot, Second stop

Never thought that
>Better stop that, Clever combat, Get a contact, Settle contract

News at eight
>Blues and hate, Boo the stage, Choose to hate, Crew is late, Dues are paid, Lose the race, Through the gate, Who's the greatest

News at nine
>Do the time, Drew the line, Lose the time, Shoes are mine, View is fine

News at ten
>Choose the men, Do again, Use the pen, Use some sense

News release
>Amuse the people, Choose the beat, Clues are weak, Reuse the beat, Through the week

New and improved
>Choose not to lose, Few of them choose, Losing the groove, Sue and get sued, Using the moves, Who gets the dues

New school
>Loose tool, Too cruel, Two fools, Who's cool

Next in line
>Best design, Check the time, Dressed to shine, Every time, Guessed it right, Guest of mine, Just in time, Let's

rewind, Never sign, Rest of time, Test of time

Night club
Fight drugs, Hike up, I could, Light plug, Might struggle

No chance
Blow sand, Both hands, Low lands, No man, Throw sand, Won't dance

No comment
Choke on it, Flow vomit, No content, Slow onset, So modest, Spoke honest

No dice
Go thrice, Go twice, Go wide, Low price, Low tide, No pride, So iced, So nice, So wide, Throw rice, Toe sliced,

No limit
Cope with it, Don't finish, Flows mimicked, Go in it, No minute, So spin it, So timid, Though is it

No wait
Don't hate, Don't say it, Locate, Low rate, Notate, Okay, So great, So late, Won't take

Nonsense
Constant, Got tense, Long fence, Lost sense, Onset

Northern light
Border's tight, Colder night, For tonight, Storm tonight, Stormy night

Nose bleed
Flow's weak, No need, No seed, Slow beat, Slow speed, So sweet

Not a problem
Got me galling, Got them all in, Got to solvent, Top of all them

Note to self
Flow as well, Flow is hell, Go to hell, Hope to help, Lower shelf

Not fair

Got dared, Got scared, Hot air, Stop where, Talk there, Top pair, Walk there

Nothing to see

Anomaly, Jump to the beat, Other than me, Something for free, The nominee

Notice the difference

Closer than distant, Close to deliverance, Flow isn't dissonant, Know in an instance, Nobody listened, So is the dissonance, Though it is dissonant

No time

Dope rhyme, Flow rhymes, Know why, No shine, No sign, Oh my, So fine, Won't find

Notorious

It's spurious, So furious, So glorious, Victorious

Not to mention

Got attention, Got protection, Got the pension, Lots of tension, Stop infection, Stop the tension, Taught the lesson, Top attention

Now or never

Bow together, How's the weather, Loud and clever, Ours better, Power getter, Shout together

Number One

Summer fun, Was begun, Was undone

Number game

Gust of flame, Just became, Others claim, Other day, Other way, Summer rain, Under came, Under pain, Was the same

Number two

Coming through, Other shoe, Other tune, Some for you, Under you, Wonder who

Number three
>Come to be, Fun to be, Lunch for free,
>Under siege, Under me

Nursery rhymes
>Earth is aligned, First is the line,
>First to resign, Hurting the mind

Nuts and bolts
>Custom sold, Dust the old, Luster
>folds, Must behold, What unfolds

Obey the law
>Don't waste it all, Flow pace is raw, No space to crawl, Okay to fall, Won't take the call

Obstacle course
>Got some remorse, Hospital source, Off in the forest, Off with the horse, Optical force, Possible force, Shot in the tors<u>o</u>

Off my chest
>All the best, <u>A</u> lot is left, Cause a mess, Fought the west, Lost the best, Lost the bet, Not forget, Toss the best

Off the chain
>Cough in pain, Cost to play, Not as plain, Pause and play, Talk of fame

Off the wall
>Caught the ball, Cross the hall, Drop the call, Fought them all, Stop the call

Old dog, new tricks
>No thoughts to spit, So got news quick, So hot it's sick

Old school
>Bold fool, Cold pool, Old rule, Stroll through

On the edge
>Call the feds, Drop the wedge, Got to pledge, Off the ledge, Pop the meds, Stop the dredge

Open minded

Globalize it, Hope to find it, Know what time is, Overwrite it, So divided

Open road

Broken code, Broke the code, Choke the throat, Nose to nose, Soak the load, Throw the rope

Open season

Cope with treason, Show the beacon, Though the reason

Open up shop

Choke and then drop, Go for the spot, Know that it's hot, Lower the top, Over the top

Optical illusion

Constable's intruding, Constantly excusing, Continental fusion, Hospital infusion, Obstacle elusion, Offering exclusion, Possible intrusion

Organized crime

Born to fight crime, Born to write rhymes, More than five times, Sort of high time

Out of luck

Bow and up, Down the flood, Loud enough, Powder puff, Shout it up

Out of reach

How to cheat, How to speak, Louder screech, Power speech, Sound is cheap, Sound or peep

Out of the way

Down to the bay, Hour and wage, How do I say, Power is great, Shower today

Overflow

Go below, Going slow, Hope to go, Know the code, Open show, Overload, Solo show

Overnight

Flow is tight, Go inside, Know the rights, Overwrite, Shone a light, So polite, Throw the mic

Overpower

Flow devours, Open hours, Shows an hour, Sober shower, Throw the flowers

Over react

Go in the back, Know as a fact, Odor is bad, Opening act, Open the back, Sober up fast

Overtime

Flow is tight, Go inside, Know in time, Know the rights, Overwrite, Shone a light, Show the line, So polite, Throw the mic, Wrote the rhyme

Oxygen mask

Boss of the class, Cost all the cash, Hospital cast,
Hospital pass, Lost in the last, Toss in the back

Painkiller
> Brain filler, Change giver, Drain rivers, Game winner, Lame singer, Make thinner

Paradise
> Air and ice, Hair and lice, Memorize, Pair of eyes, Sterilize, Terrorize

Parole officer
> A known obstacle, That's so possible, The whole hospital

Party time
> Are behind, Are in line, Part of mine, Saw the sign, Smarter mind

Pass the bottle
> Back to sorrow, Path to follow, Smash the throttle, That's tomorrow, Track is hollow

Pass the mic
> At the sight, Back inside, Crack is white, Crack of light, Fasten tight, Flash it bright, Flash the light, Smash the pride, That's denied, Track is tight

Pave the way
> Aces played, Break away, Chase away, Great array, Made the day, Making way, Paid to say, Pay to play, Play to play, Rain today, Save the day

Pay back

Blame that, Hey that, Maybach, Payback, Play at, Playback, Say that, They rap, Weigh that

Pay to play

Aces played, Break away, Chase away, Great array, Made the day, Making way, Paid to say, Pay to play, Play to play, Rain today, Save the day

Pedal to the metal

Better on a level, Get another medal, Meddle in the kettle, Nettle to a level, Never to be settled

Peer pressure

Hear lectures, Near jester, Sheer texture, We're fresher

Pen strokes

Enclosed, Encode, Gemstone, Hemp rope, Lens poked, Send hope, Then spoke

Pen to the paper

Bended and tapered, Lending a favor, Sending an angel, Senses the laser, When it is later

Perfect rhyme

Burning lines, Earn a dime, Girl is fine, Learn the lines, Worth the time

Period

Delirious, Myriad, Serious

Peripheral vision

A little addition, Horrific collision, I'm with the decision, The critic's incision, To finish the mission,

P.G. 13

Beat is bursting, Be real thirsty, Be the first thing, Keep it surging, Keep on urging

P.H.D.

Be lately, Cheap safety, He ate three, Need A.C., See a dream, She hates me, She's eighteen

Photograph

Don't know that, Explode the blast, Hope for that, Know the facts, Loaded fast, Posing as, Show the cash, Solo act

Picture that

Diction's bad, Fiction's whack, Lick the cat, Mix and match, Quick and fast, Rich with cash, Thick and fat, Which is that, Witch's bag

Picture this

Figured it, Flick the wrist, Hit and miss, Listen quick, Pitch to miss

Piece of mind

Beach and sky, Cheat and lie, Feast tonight, Fiend of mine, Release the rhyme

Piggyback

Give me that, Gritty track, Hit me back, Kitty cat, Mini track, Pity that, Sit in back, Witty crack

Pins and needles

Fill the diesel, Hit the weasel, Kings and Caesars, Since the Beatles, With the measles

Plasma screen

Act obscene, Ask a fiend, Back and lean, Cash is green, Fast and mean, Pass the cream, Tag the dream

Plastic wrap

Blast a rap, Catch the rat, Fast to catch, Last to clap, Last to laugh, Master that

Platinum status
Act a bit lavish, Fasten the, Faster than fastest, That is a habit

Play by play
Again today, A game to play, A later day, And sail away, A place to stay, Day by day, Make the play, So say my name, Take away, The main array, To stay away

Play the field
Chase the, Make a deal, Make me feel, Make the wheel, Waste the meal

Plead guilty
Deal's nifty, Deal's shifty, Feel filthy, Heed quickly, Need fifty, Need sixty, Read with me

Plea for help
Deal is dealt, Feed yourself, Feel the wealth, Freedom's felt, People felt, Seed is dealt, See the wealth

Please believe
Be the lead, Feed the greed, Feel the grief, Need to bleed, People free, People leave

Point it out
Boys are loud, Join me now, Join the count, Poison cloud

Point of no return
Choice is how we learn, Choice is no concern, Poison doesn't burn

Polo shirt
Don't go search, Go-go work, Oh so mirth, Show no mirth, Show no worth, Won't go first

Pole position
Cold and missing, Flow collision, Flow is missing, No decision, No one listens, Solo mission, So's the vision

Popular demand

Got the first again, Not a perfect plan, Shock and surge the land, Stopped and turned and ran

Power drill

Down the pill, Lounge and chill, Sound is ill

Power play

Cowards say, Crown away, Down the way, Found the way, Sounds amazing

Predictable

A spectacle, Delectable, Detectable, Impeccable, It's getable, Replicable, Selectable

Present the case

A mental state, Demented rate, Presence is great, Resent and hate, The pencil states

Priceless

Lifeless, Slice this, White lips, Write this

Price to pay

Find a way, Guide the way, Like to play, Pride and pain, Quite a day, Ride away, Wide array

Private property

Life is obsolete, Rhymes are wobbly, Why's it possibly, Write it properly, Write it sloppily

Proceed with caution

It's free to auction, Receive the option, The beat is awesome, The streets are locked in

Produce the beat

And choose to speak, And shoot the heat, It's news to me, Reduce the heat, Then cruise the streets, The truth is weak

Prototype
>Flow so tight, Show no fright, Solo fight, Throw no strikes

Proud to be
>Around the tree, Astounded me, Bound to see, Loud and free, Out of me, Out of reach

Public enemy
>But I'll let it be, Double when it's free, Love to get a beat, Rubble and debris, Subtle

Put it down
>Could've drowned, Good for now, Should've found

Pyrotechnic
>I'm corrected, I will pledge it, Lines are septic, Lines connected, Rhymes infected, Ride and wreck it, Why correct it

Qualified
> All abide, Bona fide, Call denied, Homicide, Starry eyed

Quarterback
> Force it back, For the track, Hordes and packs, Lord of rap, Order that, Sort of whack

Question mark
> Chest and heart, Just an art, Lesson starts, Session starts, Set the spark

Quick fix
> Gimmicks, Hit splits, Mimics, Misfits, Mix nix, Spit sick, Split tricks, With sticks

Quicksand
> Big man, Kick sand, Mix-stand, Nix chance, Pick hands, Spit , This dance, With plans

Quit on the spot
> Isn't a lot, Kick it and talk, Pick up and spot, Spit on the top

Quote that
> Blow past, Coat rack, Flow fast, Grow fast, No practice, Slow track, Spoke back, Throw back

Race past

Ace that, Chase fast, Great rap, Laced track, Playback, Racetrack, Take back, Take that, Taste bad, Waste that

Rags to riches

At the limit, Chapter's finished, Last to finish, That's ballistic, That's the business, Track's diminished

Rain down

Break out, Fade out, Great sound, Make proud, Make sound, Play now, Race out, Same sound, Same town, Take out

Raise the bar

Chase the car, Chasing stars, Play the bar, Play the card, Take it far, Way we are

Ransom money

Answer dummy, Dancing funny, Fans are running

Rap circles around

Brats working it out, That's lurking about, That's perfected now, That's permanent now

Ray of light

Game is tight, Laser strike, Make it right, Rain tonight, Razor tight, Say I might, Stay the night, Take the mic

Razor sharp

Ace of cards, Major art, Make it far, Praying hard, Raining hard, Take the part

Reach the finish
>Freedoms limit, Keep the gimmick, Need a minute, Speech is mimicked

Read between the lines
>Cheat deceit and lies, Keep the sequence right, Need the beat to rhyme, Need the piece of mind, See it in your eyes

Read over
>Be sober, Feet odor, <u>Four</u> leaf clover, Free loner, Speak lower

Real life
>Beat's tight, Feel like, Heed light, Keep right, Realize, Speak right, Steal lines

Recent news
>Beat ensues, Decent shoes, Feel the blues, Need to use, Speed and cruise

Recite the lines
>Incite the rhymes, Inside the mind, It's dynamite, Rewind the mind, This time it's right

Reckless endangerment
>Endless and dangerous, Just to create the best, Restless and slanderous, Testing is dangerous

Recover fast
>A hovercraft, Another trap, A thunder clap, Discover that, The summer passed, Uncover facts

Recover quickly
>My brother's with me, The others tricky, To hover swiftly

Red Cross
>Bets off, Checked off, Fresh frost, Get lost, Get tossed, Head's lost, Just pause, Set off

Red eyes

Bedside, Beside, Demise, Less time, Tell lies, Westside

Reduce to rubble

But two is double, Confused and fuddled, Ensues in trouble, It's loose and subtle, Just blew some bubbles

Regret to say

Detect the pain, Neglect and hate, Select the same, We get insane

Regulate

Educate, Elevate, Emulate, Escalate, Meditate, Set it straight, Yesterday

Relentless

Defenseless, It's senseless, It tenses, The senses, This sentence, With lenses

Remember the time

December the nine, Descendant in line, Resend and remind, The fence is on fire, The sentences rhyme

Rendezvous

All the clues, Crawling through, Follow through, Got it through, Got to do, On to you, Want to do

Repeat it again

But people amend it, Defeated it then, Reread it and then, The secret has ended, To lead with a pen

Replaced with

Defaced it, Erased it, He aced it, She aced it, The faceless, We aced it

Represent

Best defense, Detriment, Element, Eminent, Reverent, Sentiment

Reputation

Emulation, Escalation, Estimation, Regulation, Speculation

Rest the case
Bet the ace, Debt to pay, Estimate, Gets erased, Has to wait, Hesitate, Lets debate, Set the pace, Test the bass, Ventilate

Retrospect
Echoes less, Get respect, Get so wet, Head so wrecked, Then protect, Velcro vest

Revelation
Animation, Elevation, Estimation, Generation, Hesitation, Meditation, Preparation, Separation

Rewrite it
Delighted, Incited, Recited, Recite it, Reminded, Rewind it

Rhetorical question
Historical lecture, Immoral intention, Important protection

Ricochet
In a day, Inner hate, It's OK, Kiss away, Lift away, Little late, Sit and play

Riddle this
Bigger hits, Fiddle with, Flip the lip, Hit and miss, Little bit, Middle lip, With a kiss

Ride it out
By the pound, Cried about, Find it out, Lights are out, Mind the sound, Strike it down, Tried it out, Wider now, Write it down

Ride the wave
Brighter day, Find a way, Hide away, Like to say, Night to day, Right of way, Time to play, Try to say

Right now
> Bite down, Find out, Lights out, Nightgown, Strike down, White out, Wipe out

Right to left
> Hide the mess, Life is blessed, Life's a test, Like it less, Try to help, Write the best

Ring of fire
> Been a while, Give a smile, In a while, Is in style, Little tired, Simple life, Single child

Rip in half
> Chips are stacked, Insist that, In the bag, It's a fact, Lifted back, List the facts, Missing that, This or that, With a blast, Witness that

Rise and fall
> Climb the wall, Kind of small, Might recall, Tried it all, Tylenol

Roadblock
> Don't stop, Flow's hot, Load off, No stop, Shows stop, So hot, Won't stop

Road kill
> Flow's ill, Low chill, No frills, No skill, No will, Show skills, So ill

Road trip
> Flow with, Glow stick, Low whip, No tricks, Shows it, Won't stick

Rock and roll
> Bought a soul, Dominoes, Drop and fold, Got it sold, Hot and cold

Rock the boat
> Got promoted, Got the flow, Lots of dough, Stop the show, Stop to float

Rock the cradle
> Got a favor, Not disabled, Not enabled, Off the table, Shock the cable

Rock the mic
Drop the knife, Got the light, Lost a life, Posh and high <u>class</u>, Talk or fight, Talk tonight

Role model
Flow's hotter, Full throttle, Grow bothered, No bother, Whole bottle

Roll of quarters
Bold and older, Colder shoulder, <u>Control</u> the border, No disorder, Sold the order, Storm is colder

Root of the problem
Music is awesome, Truth isn't shocking, Who isn't talking

Run away
Come a day, Come and play, Come and stay, One a day, Summer day, Underway

Run of the mill
Come for the thrill, Drum beat is ill, From and until, Some other will, Sun up until

Rush the stage
Brushed away, Crush the rage, Flushed away, Jump the page, Love to hate, Luster fades, Underage, What's the name

Rusty nail
Bust a nail, Must prevail

Sacred right
>Late at night, Make it right, Play it right, Play tonight Take the mic

Salt and pepper
>All is better, Autumn weather, Fall like feathers

Same as before
>Arrange on the floor, Paving the floor, Making it roar, Name on the door, Phase one to four

Sand paper
>Blank laser, Chance taker, Hand shaker, Plan changer, Trance breaker

Saturday
>Back away, Fast to say, Latter day, Mad and hate, Rap away, That a way

Save a life
>Chase the light, Say the wise, Say tonight

Save the day
>Change today, Chase away, Insane and sane, Pave the way, Race away, Wait okay

Say that again
>Gave back the pen, Gave that a ten, Play that again, Take back to them

Scapegoat
>Ache so, Fake flow, May know, Late show, Take jokes, Take no, Tape closed, Way low

Scatter around
>As it was found, Rap to the sound, Shackled and bound, Shackle the ground, Tackle it down, Trap in the sound

Scrape it up
>Break it up, Hate it but, Make it cut, Make enough, Make it flood, Play in mud, Saying what, Shake the club, Take a cut

Scratch the surface
>Act like shirkers, Ask the circus, Backs are shirtless, Back to working, Practice perfect

Scream in pain
>Cleaned away, Feel the rain, Feel the same, Lead away, Need to pay, Plead and pray, Scene'll change, Seems the same, Seen the same

Scream it loud
>Beat around, Even out, Feel about, Obscene but proud, See without

Screws loose
>Chew through, Choose too, Choose truce, New to, New view, View through, Who's who

Seal it off
>Being soft, Cheat the law, Even cost, Feeling lost, Mean and awful, Need a coffee, Need to cough

Self defense
>Felt the tension, Fence to fence, Held the pencil, Pens and pencils, Tend to sense

Self made
>Bells play, Best rate, Best way, Checkmate, Help came, Less great, Rent's paid, Send aid

Sell out

Fell down, Get out, Less doubt, Spell out, Yell out

Sentence structure

Hands'll rupture, Meant to fluster, Menace blusters, Tension punctures

Separated

Decorated, Elevated, Generated, Hesitated, Meditated, Renegade, Serenaded, Venerated

Set an example

Get all the vandals, Get from an angle, Getting entangled, Having to cancel, Letting them sample, Set at the ankle

Set the bar

Get the car, Getting far, Spread it far, Sweating hard

Set the pace

Better days, Bet the ace, Detonate, Elevate, Escalate, Feather weight, Get erased, Hesitate, Levitate, Meditate, Separate

Several times

Better than mine, Clever and bright, Ethical crimes Federal crimes, General rhymes, Leverage lines, Medical, Set up the rhymes

Sever an artery

Bet on the lottery, Get a ménage a three, Get in mahogany, Get in the harmony, Get them to start to see, Settle in harmony, When it is hard to be

Shake it off

Ache a lot, Blame it all, Making lots, Stray and lost, Take a loft, Taking lots

Shattered dreams

Bad and obscene, Batter the fiend, Catch a gleam, Master these, Scatter the scene,

Shattered glass

Acting fast, After that, Chatter back, Flabbergast, Gasp aghast, Happens fast, Magic act, Pass the class, Rapid fast, Rap a track

Shock absorber

Block the border, Fought disorder, Got the order, Locked and cornered, Stop as ordered, Stop informers

Shock the crowd

Knock them out, Lock it out, Not about, Not as loud, Shop around, Stomp and shout, Stop the sound

Shockwaves

Blockade, Crop maze, Got paid, Got paved, Got saved, Lost days, Not saved, Top ways

Shoe laces

Glue's pasted, New places, Through places, To face it, Two aces, Two faces

Shoe string

Few sing, Mood swing, New things, New ring, Two things

Shook up

Cook up, Hooked up, Look up, Took up

Show a sign

Below the line, Flow and rhyme, Glow and shine, Rope and tie, So is mine

Showtime

No sign, Dope rhyme, Flow lines, Flow rhymes, Know why, No shine, No sign, Oh my, So fine, Won't find

Show up
    Blow up, Go nuts, Grow up, Know what,
    No what, Slow up, So what, Throw up,
    Toe up
Shut down
    But now, Cut down, Cut out, Cut sound,
    Lucks out, Must frown, Must now, Sucks
    now, Sundown, Uptown

Sickening
    Bickering, Dithering, Finishing, Fit
    them in, Listening, Slithering,
    Thickening, Tinkering
Sicker rhymes
    Hit rewind, Isn't time, It is time,
    Since the time, Single lines, Wicked
    times, With the lines
Sigh of relief
    Fire up the heat, Lie in defeat, Rhyme
    on the street, Shine on the beat, Tie
    up the feet
Sign the contract
    Find the contact, I just got that, Line
    to combat, Rhyme is on track
Silence the crowd
    Find a way out, Guiding the sound,
    Style is renowned, Violent and loud
Silent night
    Ultraviolet light, Violent fight,
    Violet light, While I write
Simple life
    Twinkle light, Hypnotize, In a while,
    In disguise, Inner child, Is in style,
    Mystify, Simple life, Single file,
    Twinkle eyes
Sing a song
    In the dawn, In the pond, Is it wrong,
    Linger on, Sing along, With a bond,
    With it on

Sinister

Is sicker, It's twister, Lip shifter, Minister, With blisters

Sit back down

In that town, It's that sound, Lips strapped down, Pick that sound, Rip that out, This rap crown

Sit up straight

Become great, Interstate, Is contained, It's untamed, This update

Six pack

Bit that, Knick knack, Lip smack, Miss that, Rip back, Slim fast, Wish that

Sixteen bars

Hit restart, In dream cars, Lip sync songs

Skid to a stop

Hid at the spot, Hit up the spot, Isn't a lot, Lid's off the top, Listen to songs, Mix in a shock

Skin burn

Insert, Insured, Intern, In third, In turn, Linger, Pick first, Singer, Winter

Skip the beat

History, Hit the streets, Mystery, Shift the feet, Trip the feet, With defeat

Skyrocket

Eye socket, My pocket, Time clock it

Sleep on it

Be conscious, Be honest, Be modest, Be taunted, Recharge it, See saw it

Slice it up

Dice it up, Life is tough, Tight and shut, Try the luck, Write enough, Write it up

Slip up
> Fizz up, Hic up, Hit up, Lick up, Lit up, Pick up, Rip up, Stick up, Tip up, Zip up,

Slow it down
> Below the ground, Flow's profound, Go around, Go to town, Open now

Slow zone
> Flow's phoney, Go home, Home grown, Low tone, No clone, Own clone, Postpone, Throw stones

Smack down
> Act out, Bad count, Last round, Max out, Pass out, That's loud,

Small time
> All kind, All mine, All rhymes, Call sign, Star sign, Wall climb,

Smash the bottle
> Back to toddle, Blast the throttle, Latch the toggle, That's a bother

Smash to pieces
> Grab and seize it, Last is weakest, Pack up beat it, Rap deceases, Tag and he's it, Tag and she's it, That conceited, Track just ceases

Smoke rings
> Boasting, Choking, Don't sing, Grow wings, Joking, Most wins, Soaking, Throw things, Won't sing

Snake eyes
> Brake lights, Late night, Make lies, Paint dries, Play dice, Take sides

Snakeskin
> Break in, Great things, Make things, Shaking, Wade in

Sneak peak
> Beats leak, Beats speak, Free beat, Heat seek, Knees weak, Please keep, Sweet cheek

Sneak up
> Free but, Knees cut, Retouch, Speak up, Street guts, Teacup

Snowstorm
> Blow horns, Grow cold, Grow old, Low roar, No form, No more, So short, So warm

Some time
> Crunch time, Dumb rhyme, Lunch line, One line, Punch line, Runs fine

Sound effects
> Found a cent, How's the rest, Loud and dense, Now again, Now the next, Round the bend, Shout the text, Sound's annexed, Sounds intense

Sneak preview
> Heat seek through, He's see through, Leech bleeds you, She's see through, We see you

Speakers blasting
> Beat and thrashing, Beats are clashing, Heat is flashing, Keep it lasting, People asking, People laughing, Speech is raspy, Speech is scratchy, Weeks are passing

Speak slower
> Be sober, Free flower, Keep lower, Leap over, Street mower, Street poser

Speak up
> Be stuck, Cheeks cut, Deep cut, Free stuff, See what, Speed up, Teacup

Spell it out
> Belly down, Head is clouded, Melting down, Said about, Selling out, Tell about, Well without,

Spice it up
> Dice it up, Eyes are shut, Slice and cut, Spike the punch

Spill the beans
> Fill the scene, Ill and clean, Kill the dreams, Steal the scene, Still to see

Spit fire
> Bit tired, Get wired, In spirals, It's vital, Retire, Sit higher, With style

Spit shine
> Fistfight, Fix mine, It's fine, Pick mine, Sick rhymes, Skintight, Slick rhyme, This high, This time, Which line, With rhymes

Split in half
> Listen fast, Lit the blast, Rip and blast, Sit and bask, Spit the acid, With the cash, With the mask

Split the profit
> Different sauces, In the closet, Lift the coffin, Missed and lost it, Quick to stop it, This is toxic, Tip the pockets, With precaution

Split the track
> Lips are chapped, Lips are fastened, Lit the blast, Spill some acid, Spit the rap, Spit it rapid

Spoil the surprise
> Boys in disguise, Choice is denied, Join in the ties, Point to the skies, Poison the mind, Toy with the mind

Spotlight
> Got tight, Hot light, Hot night, On time, Stop sign, Taught right, Wrong line, Wrong time

Still standing
> Disbanding, Enchanting, Is landing, Spill sand in, With candy

Stack it up
> Back it up, Bag a nut, Pack it up, Rack it up, Slash and cut, That is luck

Stand up
Can't trust, Hands up, Hang up, Land floods, Man up, Slam shut

Start the ride
Charter flight, Heart's denied, Part the side, Starry sky, Stars tonight

Status quo
Afterglow, Ask to go, Last to know, Laugh and joke, Rap it slow, Rap the flow, Stack it low, That's the show

Stay awake
Change the fate, Change the pace, Late today, Make them wait, Plague and ache, Take a day

Stick to the plan
Is in demand, Rip like a fan, Spit like a man, This is the chance

Stomp the ground
Dawn to now, Drop the sound, Flaunt around, Gone for now, Got the crowd, Jump around, Song is loud, Taunt around, Yawn around

Stomp the yard
All the cards, Fought it hard, Got the card, Off the guard

Stop the music
Dropped to ruins, Got abusive, Got confusing, Got to prove it, Not amusing, Not to lose it

Stop to think
Block the ink, Hot in pink, Lost a wing, Not a thing, On the brink, Stop and sink

Straight ahead
Ace the test, Ate the lead, Break a leg, Make a bet, Pay a debt

Straight down
Break out, Great sound, Make proud, Make sound, Race out, Take out

Straight jacket
> Fake plastic, Great tactics, Make racket, Take action, Takes practice

Street smart
> Beat start, Cheap parts, Street car, Streets talk, Weak heart, Weak start

Strictly speaking
> In a meeting, Itchy feeling, Lips are leaking, Quickly leaving, Tricks deceiving

Strike a pose
> I suppose, Slightly closed, Style and flows, Tighter flows, Write a prose

Strike down
> Bite down, Buy now, My town, Right now, Slight sound, Time's out, Wind down, Write down

Struck down
> Cut down, Duck down, Dumb clown, Lucked out, Must pound, Must sound, Uncrown, Uptown

Stumble and fall
> Jump in the car, Jungle is small, Humble and small, Rubble and all, Rupture it all, What is the call

Sucker punch
> Luck is struck, Pump it up, Up in front, Upper cut, What's for lunch, What's this junk

Suffer more
> Bust the door, Off the floor, Other door, Underscore, What's the score

Sum it up
> Coming up, Dumb enough, Hummer truck, One's enough, Running up, Thunder struck, Uppercut, What is up, Wonder what, Won the cup

Sunday

Come stay, Gunplay, Monday, Mundane, Someday, Some say, Some way

Sunshine

Fun rhyme, Fun times, Lunch line, Punch line, Run mine, Sometime, Sunshine, Unwind, Won mine

Supercharged

Loot the car, Stoop as far, Super star, Truth is hard, Who's in charge

Superman

Do a dance, Lose the chance, Lose a grand, Newer plans, Super man, Through the fans, Who's the man

Surge of power

Hurts the coward, Nerves are sour, Search for hours, Worse than ours

Surround sound

And found out, Around town, From ground down, The gown's down

Survival of the fittest

Decided in a minute, The vital are statistics, The writing is simplistic

Survive the storm

And wipe the floor, A nice reward, From five to four, Inside the store

Sweep the floor

Beats galore, Be forlorn, Feet are sore, Keep the form, Leave the door, Leeches bore, Need some more

Sweet as candy

Beach is sandy, Be demanding, Being antsy, Keep it fancy, Keep on standing

Sweet sorrow

Beats borrowed, Be followed, Be hollow, We are though

Sweeten the deal
> Eat up the meal, Freedom will heal, Heat up the steel, Heat up the wheels, Keeping it real

Switch the style up
> Digits dialed up, Rip the wildest, Spit the bile up, Without my luck

Syllable
> Biblical, Critical, Liberal, Literal, Miracle, Physical, Pinnacle

Synthesize
> Hypnotize, In disguise, Inner child, Mystify, Simple life, Twinkle eyes

Systematic
> Bit dramatic, Interactive, In the attic, It's a tactic, It's elastic, It's fantastic, Just a spastic, With the addicts

Tailor made
> Fail to play, Fail to say, Hail will raid, Sail away, Stale and fade, Take a break

Take a break
> Ace of bass, Change the fate, Face to face, Face the fate, Hate to hate, Make or break, Paste the face, State to state

Take a chance
> Change the plans, Changing hands, Later plans, Make demands, Make it dance, Table dance

Take a minute
> Fake and mimicked, Make a gimmick, Pay the ticket, Wait to finish

Take an order
> Breaks the shoulder, Make disorder, Pay the quarter, Shake the boulder

Take it out
> Break it out, Hate to shout, Lay it out, Make the sound, Play it loud, Say about, Say it loud, Spray the crowd, Stay without

Take five
> Breaks ice, Fake eyes, Fake I.<u>D.</u>, <u>Forsake</u> lives, Great size, Make lies, Play nice

Tamper with
Answer this, Cancel it, Cancer stick, Candles lit, Handle it, Ramble it, Stand or sit

Tantalizing
Analyzing, And defying, And denying, Plans arising, Plan designing Scandalizing, Stand the lying, Vandalizing

Tap dance
Advance, Backhand, Bad chance, Lap dance, Last chance, Last man, Rap stance

Tape record
Break the cord, Break the door, Making more, May get bored, Rain and pour, Shake the floor, Take the gold, Taking hold

Target practice
All in plastic, Aren't as drastic, Arson action, Cars are stacking, Hardly active, Part's attractive, Smartest tactic

Task at hand
As a man, Ask to dance, Crack the can, Last demand, Master plan, That's the plan,

Taste this
Aces, Bassist, Cases, Place it, Places, Shameless, Straight miss, Take with, Wasted

Technique is flawless
And freedom causes, And keep it modest, Just being honest, Repeat then pause it

Telephone
Bless the home, Get a bone, Left alone, Mellow tone, Never know, Set the tone

Television

Demolition, Get a vision, Get commission, Get permission, Head collision, Premonition

Temporary

Contemporary, Getting scary, Have to bury, Secondary, Sedentary

Tempting

Attempting, Best thing, Empty, Plenty, Presenting, Renting, Sending, Sensing, Tensing

Terrified

Electrified, Petrified, Sterilize, Terrorize

Test of time

Best to rhyme, Fresh and fine, Guessed it right, Guest of mine, Have to find, Lesson five, Rest is fine

Test the water

Best is hotter, Better offer, Get the dollar, Have to holler, Left the caller, Pest and bother, Rest the collar

Thanks again

Make amends, Shake the hand, Take a stand, Taste the end, Waste the pen

That's a wrap

Battle back, Battle tactics, Crack the bat, Master that, Rap attack, That's a fact

That's the truth

After you, Ask for proof, Battle truce, Pack is loose, Rats are loose

That's what they say

After the rain, After today, Half is okay, Last of the day, Master the brain, Passing away, Practice to play, Rap is a game

The devil's calling

A feather's falling, I'll bet them all in, The level's falling, The pedal's falling, The weather's swapping

The tables turn

A fate is learned, My face is stern, The game is burned, What's made is earned

Think about it

In accounting, It amounted, Sing around it, Sink and drowning, Stinks astounding

Think outside the box

Sing out by the block, Sink down like a rock, Sit down while I talk, This sound hypes the block, Without time to stop

This is honesty

It is possibly, Rip it awesomely, Spill the gossipy, Still a colony, This apology, Wish it onto me, With psychology

Through the wire

Lose a tire, Moving higher, To aspire, To retire

Throw fire

Flow's higher, Grow tired, Know why, No liar, Rope tighter, So wired

Throw me off

Flow is hot, Flow is soft, Know the boss, Low and soft, Over toss, Sober thought

Throw strikes

Flow tight, Glow lights, Go write, Know why, No light, So right, So tight

Thunder clap

Coming back, Run it back, Run the pack, Summer track, Tougher pack, Under that

Thursday
>Birthplace, First day, First way, Worse way

Tick tock
>Click clock, Criss cross, Hip hop, Hit stop, Pick locks, This spot, This stops, Tip top

Time is ticking
>Crime is sinking, Minds remitting, Rhyme is spitting, While I'm thinking, Whine and kicking

Times are hard
>Find the start, Find the heart, Finer art, I depart, Kind of far, Like a dart, Night's are dark, Rhyme's an art, Sides apart

Tired of that
>Desire to rap, Fire it back, Guided it back, Higher than that, Style is back

Tolerated
>All are rated, Automated, Confiscated, Dominated, Fall and break it, Got abated, Nominated, Not debated, Obligated, Oscillated, Populated

Top speed
>Got need, Hot beat, Not see, Posses, Soft breeze, Stop please

Top that
>Got back, Hop back, Hot track, Lost fast, Not mad, Not whack, Shot back, Talk back, Top hat, Top stack

Toss and turn
>Boss is first, Bought the first, Cost to earn, Got a surge, Lost and burned, Not the urge

Track down
>Bad crowd, Back out, Bad sound, Cash cow, Cash out, Class clown, Last count,

Mad now, Mass crowd, Sad frown, That's vowed

Train wreck

Breakneck, Came went, Main deck, Make bets, May get, Paycheck, Plain set, Rain wet, Same set

Treason

Beacon, Lesion, Reason, Season, Teasing, Weaken,

Trick it out

Chicken out, Fit the sound, Live without, Sing it loud, Still about, Think and doubt, Whip around, With a crown

Trip and fall

Hit the ball, In the wall, It's a ball, Limp and crawl, Middle stall, Miss a call, Tick them off, With a doll, With them all

Triple play

Inner hate, In the day, In the hay, Minute rate, Single day, Sin or pray, Sit and stay, Think and wait

Trip out

Dip down, In doubt, Is proud, Pick out, Think out, This loud, Whip out, With clout, Without

Troublemaker

Another favor, Become a traitor, Bubble breaker, Couple breaker, Cuts a razor, Cut the paper, Double taker, Shut the hater, Wasn't greater

True or false

Do or halt, Lose it all, Stoops and falls, Threw the salt, Through the walls, To the mall, Two missed calls, Use your balls

Trust that
> Bust back, Crush that, Cut bad, Must rap, Rush back, Shut back, Tough pack

Trust this
> Busted, Just miss, Rush with, Rusted, Touch with, What's this

Truth be told
> Blues are cold, Choose the gold, Choose to fold, Loosen bolts, New and old, Ruthless cold

Tuesday
> Blue face, Do say, Few say, Mood sway, New day, Too late, True way, Who say

Turn it down
> Burning sound, Burn it down, Curtains down, Earn a pound, Search around, Surge of sound, Turn around

Turn it up
> Burn and cut, Curtains up, Earn enough, Search and bust

Turn up the bass
> Certainty makes, Curtains are raised, Burned and erased, Burn up the way, Search every place, Surgery table, Verse is a waste, Worse than today

Twilight
> Bite size, By night, Eyesight, Fly by, Hindsight, I might, Limelight, Nightlight, Shine bright, Side by, Sideline, Skylight, Why fight, Write tight

Twilight zone
> By my home, I might know, Limelight shone, Skylight shone, Why fight though

Two faced
> Choose fate, New case, New day, Room mate, Shoe lace, Shoot straight, Too late, Touché

Two handed

Loose cannon, Shoes planted, Threw sand at, Too candid, Too rancid, To stand it

Typewriter

Eyeliner, Fight fire, Hype higher, Mic tighter, Mind miner, Shine brighter, Sidewinder, Write tighter

Ultraviolet
Summertime is, Sung in silence, Sun is blinded, Underline it, Undivided

Undercover
Become another, Come discover, Dumber brother, One another, Run for cover, Shut the shutters, Sun went under

Underground
Crunch the ground, Lunge around, Stun the crowd, Thunder sound, Tons of sound, Trunk is loud, Tumble round, Upper town

Underneath
Cut is deep, Drums and beats, Some believe, Some relief, Stuttered speech, Summer heat, Unbelievable

Understand
Dumber than, Thunder slam, Wonderland, Wonder man

Undertake
Fun to make, Hunger aches, Run away, Summer day, Thunder play, Underage, Upper state

Unleashed
Bust heat, Cut teeth, Must speak, Rough speech, Run free, Run streets, Some feast, Touch screen, Tough deed, Tough streets, Un-teach

Unimportant
Come escorted, Comes imported, Cut and shorten, Not assorted, Undistorted

United

Applied it, Belied it, Decided, Defied it, Delighted, Denies it, Recited, Reminded, To hide it, To write it, Two sided

Unpleasant

Obsession, One lesson, One present, The presence

Untamed

Come rain, Fun play, Inundate, Mundane, None saved, Runway, Some came, Sun came, Tough day, Unframed, Update

Up and down

Buzzing sound, Cut around, Cut it down, Shut it down, Wasn't found

Upon impact

Along the tracks, Belong in rap, Belongs in back, It's gone in back, The song's intact

Upper class

Muster back, Must react, Thunder clap, Underpass, Under that, Wonder that

Uppercut

Buckle up, Buffer's up, Cut it up, Stuck them up, Suck a nut, Toughen up

Upper hand

Love to dance, Must demand, Other chance, Other land, Suffer man, Summer plans, Tougher man

Upright

Bus ride, Crunch time, Enough light, Just write, Lunchtime, Must find, Rough ride, Tough time, Upside, Was tight

Upside down

Bust rhymes now, But right now, Hush my sound, Must tie down, Tough time now, What's my count

Up the creek
    Cut the beat, Cut the cheek, Lust is weak, Must be sneaky, Shut the beak, Stuff is sweet, Tongue in cheek, Tough to speak, Underneath

Up the wall
    Hush them all, Luck will fall, Rush and fall, Tough to call, Wonder wall

Uptown
    Cut down, Duck down, Dumb clown, Lucked out, Must pound, Must sound, Uncrown

Urban legend
    Curse and blessing, Learn the lesson, Turn to dead ends, Turn to tension, Worth the guessing

Vacuum pack

Back to back, Hack at that, Half a pack, Pack your bag, Patch the scratch, Pat the back, Rap attack

Vaporize

Gazing eyes, Great disguise, Hate surprises, May arise, May devise, May revise, State the wise, Take a life, Take the prize, Taste the ice

Vegetate

Better rate, Decimate, Elevate, Emanate, Emulate, Enervate, Estimate, Generate, Hesitate, Levitate, Meditate, Metal plate, Said to wait, Separate

Vengeance is sweet

Ends at the beep, Ends in the street, Have to delete, Lenses are weak, Plenty to see, Sense the defeat, Sentences speak

Verse to verse

Burn the earth, Certain worth, Curse the person, Search the earth, Surf the turf, Worse and worse

Vertebrae

Burn away, Certain way, Heard them say, Impersonate, Learn a trade, Turn away

Vibe to this

Die for it, Eyes amiss, Finalist, Find it with, Rhyme is sick, Ride with it, Tidal spit

Viewfinder
New diner, Suits finer, Tooth grinder,
Two timer, Who's finer

Vindictive
Addictive, Dismissive, Inflicted,
Instinctive, Intrinsic, Is gifted, Lip
sync it, Restrictive, With split lips

V.I.P.
Behind me, Be like me, Be sky deep,
B.I.G., See I.D., She likes me

Vital sign
Cyanine, Define a rhyme, Dine and
shine, Finer line, Iodine, Refine the
line, Ride the rhyme, Time is mine,

Vital stat
Bridal bath, Deny the fact, Die for
that, Hide the rat, Lying flat, Recite
the rap

Voice is heard
Boys and girls, Choice is hers, Oil and
swerve, Point and search, Point to
search, Poison served

Voice is loud
Boys surround, Choice is clouded, Hoist
around, Point them out, Poison cloud,
Toys around

Vow to that
Crowd the back, Devour that, Now enact,
Power nap Power rap, Power track, Proud
of that, Shower cap, Sour rap, Tower
stack

Wait a little

Make a riddle, Make it jiggle, Make it
wiggle, Play the fiddle, Play the
middle, Pray to differ, Shape and
whittle, Snake'll slither, Take the
litter, Taste the spittle

Wait a minute

Bacon in it, Make the finish, Place it
in it, Play a gimmick, Race to win it,
Take the limit, Take you with it

Wait and see

A to Z, Bakery, Hate defeat, Hate on
me, Laser streak, Made to be, Play the
beat, Razor deep

Wait a second

Gave a section, Hate affection, Late
confession, Make a beckon, Safe
protection, Take a lesson, Take
direction

Wake up call

Break the wall, Hate to fall, Make the
call, May recall, Play the ball,
Straight up tall

Walk the line

Claws are grind<u>ing</u>, Flawless rhyme,
Flaws are fine, Got the time, Lost the
line, Raw as rhyme, Saw the sign, Top
to shine

Walk the other way

All the brothers say, All the others
same, Bought for mother's day, Got

above the shame, Got another name, Lost another day, Possible today, Possible to say, Stop and got the name, Stop another day

Walk the talk

Block the shot, Block to block, Draw the chalk, Got too hot, Knock the socks, Not forgotten, Rock the top, Shock and rock, Shock the flock, Stop the clock, Talk the talk, Walk the walk

Walk the walk

Block the shot, Block to block, Draw the chalk, Got too hot, Knock the socks, Not forgotten, Rock the top, Shock and rock, Shock the flock, Stop the clock, Talk the talk, Walk the walk

Wall to wall

All day long, All dissolved, All in all, All involved, All the balls, All the calls, Call the calls, Caught the fall, Crawl the halls, Stall the ball

Want it back

Got a plaque, Got attacked, Honest rap, On the track, Song is crap

Wash it down

Block in town, Boss of town, Cross the ground, Hop around, Knock it down, Toss around

Washed away

Boss today, Lost a day, Lost the play, Lost the way, Oscillate, Tossed away

Waste my time

Crazy rhyme, Erase the line, Face decline, Face the crime, Make it shine, Raise the line, Taste the lime

Watch your mouth

Bought the house, Caught without, Drop the couch, Got to doubt, Got to shout, Hot and drought, Hotter out, Pause and shout, Not about, Not as stout, Not without, Talks about

Watch your step

Bought the jet, Caught the net, Lost the bet, Not to get, Ought to bet, Sopping wet

Weather the storm

Better in form, Better informed, Feathers and thorns, Heaven is born, Settle indoors

Wednesday

Inlay, In pain, In weight, Since they, Will pay, Will play, Will stay

Weight in gold

Days of old, Hate the cold, Lake is cold, Later told, Make it bold, Wait to hold

Weight of the world

Days will unfurl, Made the head whirl, Made up of pearls, Name of the girl, Shake it and twirl

Wet and wild

Check the style, Get a trial, Get defiled, Just a mile, Just denial, Testified

What can I say

A better way, Brush it away, Busted the way, Dust it away, Just in a day, Rusted away, Suffer and pray, Up and away, Usher the lady

Whatever

Endeavor, Forever, Got severed, Surrender, That's better, Track setter

What I said

Bust ahead, But I had, Rusty lead, Shut the head, Tough to spread, Trust the dead, Trust the lead

Wherever
>Endeavour, Forever, Get clever, Then never, The weather, Whenever

Whether or not
>Better than pot, Get in the spot, Kettle is hot, Peddle the block, Settle the talk, Sever the block, Weather is hot

Whirlwind
>Cursing, First in, First win, Hurl in, Lurch in, Surfing, Surging, Thirsting, Version, Word in, Worse sin

Witch doctor
>Hip hopper, Rips hotter, Switch postures, This offer, Which shocked her

Within this track
>And spin it back, Finish the rap, It isn't that, It's in the back, Lip is attack<u>ing</u>, Pick up the plaque, Stick in the back

Within this verse
>Finish the search, Ink is dispersed, Isn't perverse, Minutes avert, Sink and immerse, Sinners converse, This is the first

Without a doubt
>Figure it out, Flip it around, Is it about, Lifted it out, Ripping it out, Rippling out, Whistle it out,

With or without
>Figure it out, Flip it around, Is it about, Lifted it out, Ripping it out, Rippling out, Whistle it out, Without a doubt

With these words
>Deep freezer, Get three thirds In reverse, Is sleeker, It's cheaper, Miss me first, This free verse

With you

Bit through, Into, It's new, It's true, Lift through, Missed too, Rip through, Slip through, Stick glue, This shoe, This view

Witness to the fact

Chilling in the back, Gifted when I rap, Hidden in the track, Hit this in the back, Listen to the rap, Sitting in the back, Slip into the glass, Whisper when I rap

Wonder what

Dumber luck, Encumbered up, Sun is up, Thunder struck, Undercut, Upper cut

Wonder why

Run the wild, Stung the eye, Summer sky, Summer time, Thunder cry, Underline, Under my

Word of the wise

Bird in the skies, Birth to demise, Earning the right, Emergency time, First in the ride, Murder the rhymes, Turn into lies, Turn to the right, Urgent this time

Words of wisdom

Blur the vision, Earn commission, Earn permission, Hurts the system, Search and missing, Turned position, Unearth a vision, Verse precision

Words that rhyme

Earth is mine, First in line, First to rhyme, Girl is fine, Verse design, World is mine, Worth the crime, Worth the time

Work around it

Curse astounded, Earth's surrounded, First to found it, Turn around and, Verses sounded

Work of art
> Burst apart, Burst the heart, First to start, Hurts the heart, Search the car

Work the block
> Dirt and rocks, Dirty socks, First to knock, First to rock, Flirt with gods, Hurl a rock, Search the block, Worth a lot

Work on it
> First on it, First sonnet, Turn honest, Words lawless, Worth modesty

World War
> Birds soar, First floor, Third door, Turn sore, Word lord, Word lore, Worse score, Worth more

Worldwide
> Birds eye, Fertile, First style, Girls cry, Shirt size, Third aisle, Turnstile, Word style, Worthwhile

World wonder
> Burst thunder, First blunder, First ponder, Her number, Turn under, Words mumbled, Word thunder

Worth a lot
> Birth's a shock, Heard the shot, Search the block, Shirt is dropped, Surging shock, Turn the top, Work the block

Worthless
> Curse it, First test, Furthest, Hurts it, Search it, Search this, Shirtless

Worthwhile
> Birds eye, Fertile, First child, First style, Girls cry, Her style, Shirt size, Third aisle, Turnstile, Word style

Wrapped around
> Ask them how, Back it down, Back to town, Blast around, Blast the sound,

Last to count, Mash the ground, Pass it out, Practice now

Wrist watch

Click clock, Criss cross, Flip flop, Hit stop, Lip locked, Pissed off, Pit stop, Thick socks, This clock, This stops, Which spot, With cops

Write a line

Bright and shine, By tonight, Dynamite, Find a dime, Find the time, Time to time, Try to rhyme

Write a verse

By the first, Fight the thirst, Hide the hurt, Kind of hurts, Like the earth, Sights invert, Why rehearse, Wide alert, Write inverse

Write it down

Bite the sound, Climb around, Like the sound, Might have found, Side of town, Tied and bound, Tie around, Wiser now

Writers block

Hyper shock, Like a dog, Like to rock, Like to talk, Pride is shot, Try to talk, Tylenol

Wrong or right

Dawn to light, Honest spite, Model life, On a night, On the flight, Song is tight

Wrong place

Long days, Long gaze, Long phase, Song plays, Songs pay, Strong bass, Wrong way

Wrong time

Long sigh, Long time, Pop flies, Song rhymes, Strong rhyme, Wrong sign

Wrong way

Long days, Long gaze, Long phase, Song
plays, Songs pay, Strong bass, Wrong
way

X-factor

Best laughter, Get after, Get tackled,
Less laughter, Next after, Next chapter

X-rated

Debated, Elevated, Just made it, Just
take it, Let's take it, Misstated,
Related, Sedated, Serrated

X-ray

Best way, Betray, Chest ray, Decay,
Delay, Essay, Get blamed, Get slain,
Just play, Next day, Next wave, Said
hey, Test aim

Xylophone

Cry alone, Find a home, Silent zone,
Time to go, Violent home, Violent prone

Year after year
>Clear up the rear, Hear that you fear, Peers I revere, Steer of the pier

Yes or no
>Best to go, Left the show, Left to know, Set to go, Test the road

Yesterday
>Best to gain, Celebrate, Escalate, Estimate, Just the pain, Just the rain, Less to pay, Less today, Rest a day, Test the way

Yo-yo
>Blow low, Go pro, No flow, No go, No-no, Oh no, Show's over, So low, Through flows

You don't know
>A low blow, And go whoa, A slow show, I won't go, So no go, Then go pro, To go home

Zebra stripes
Breathing right, Leaders fight, Leave tonight, Read the rights, Seem to like

Zero
Below, Credo, Ego, Free flow, Free show, Heat glow, Hero, Nero, <u>No</u> fear though, Please go, Weirdo

Zero gravity
Below that of me, Be so flattery, Flee and scattering, Needs no battery

Zero-to-sixty
Be sort of shifty, Heroes are missing

Zig zag
Hid at, Kick back, Lift that, Riff raff, Rip at

Zip it up
Hit a rut, Lick it up, Pick it up, Rip it up

Zoom in
Loon bin, New king, New thing, Room spin, Too grim, Too thin, Two twins

Zoom out
Flew round, New ground, New route, News shout, Shoots out, Too loud, Too proud, To shout, True doubt, Who found

Zone out
Don't pout, Don't shout, Loan out, Moan loud, No doubt, No sound, So loud, Toes out

[1, 2, 3, 4] Costello R.B. (1993). <u>The American Heritage College Dictionary</u>, Third Edition. Boston, New
York: Houghton Mifflin Company.

[5] Notorious B.I.G. *I Gotta Story to Tell*. Retrieved January 2, 2008 from WWW: http://www.lyrics.com
[6] Tupac. *Changes*. Retrieved January 2, 2008 from WWW: http://www.lyrics.com
[7] Jay Z. *Song Cry*. Retrieved January 2, 2008 from WWW: http://www.lyrics.com
[8] Nas. *The Outcome*. Retrieved January 2, 2008 from WWW: http://www.lyrics.com
[9] Bone Thugs-N-Harmony. *Crossroads*. Retrieved January 2, 2008 from WWW: http://www.lyrics.com
[10] Eminem. *Till I Collapse*. Retrieved January 2, 2008 from WWW: http://www.lyrics.com
[11] Ludacris. *Runaway Love*. Retrieved January 2, 2008 from WWW: http://www.lyrics.com
[12] Loske, B. (2004). RHYME PATTERN VARIATIONS. Retrieved December 26, 2007 from
http://www.loske.org/html/school/english/rhyme.pdf.
[13] Talib Kweli. *Get By*. Retrieved January 2, 2008 from WWW: http://www.lyrics.com

Made in the USA
San Bernardino, CA
06 December 2016